Guitar Chord Songbook

Bob Seger

Cover photo: ©Photofest

ISBN 978-1-4234-8027-3

HAL•LEONARD® CORPORATION

7777 W. BLUEMOUND RD. P.O. BOX 13819 MILWAUKEE, WI 53213

Visit Hal Leonard Online at
www.halleonard.com

Guitar Chord Songbook

Contents

Against the Wind

Words and Music by
Bob Seger

Melody:

It seems like yes-ter-day, __

G   Bm   C/G   D   Em   Am

Intro

| G | | | | |

Verse 1

    G   Bm
It seems like yesterday,   but it was long ago.

    C/G   G
Janey was lovely, she was the queen of my nights

    D   C/G
There in the darkness with the radi-o playing low. And,

    G   Bm
And the secrets that we shared,   the mountains that we moved.

    C/G   G
Caught like a wildfire out of __ control

                    C/G   D
Till there was nothing left to burn and nothing left to prove.

Pre-Chorus 1

                   Em   D   G
And I re-member what she said to me,

                         Em   C/G   G
How she swore ___ that it nev-er would end.

              Em   D   C/G
I re-member how she held ___ me, oh, ___ so tight.

                                             D
Wish I didn't know now what I didn't know then.

Chorus 1

G   Bm
Against the wind,

C/G   G
We were runnin' against the wind.

        C/G   Bm
We were young and strong,

        Am   C/G   G
We were runnin' against ____ the wind.

| | | | | |

Verse 2

G   Bm
And the years rolled slowly past,   and I found myself alone.

C/G   G
Surrounded by strangers I thought were my friends,

D   C/G
I found myself further and further from my home.

G   Bm
And I   guess I lost my way,   there were, oh, so many roads.

     C/G   G
I was living to run and running to live,

       C/G   D
Never wor - ried about paying or even how much I owed.

Pre-Chorus 2

            Em   D   G
Moving eight ____ miles a minute __ for months at a time,

            Em   C/G   G
Breaking all ____ of the rules ____ that would bend.

Em   D   C/G
I began to find myself search - ing,

                 D
Searching for shelter again __ and again.

Chorus 2

```
      G                 Bm
        Against the wind,

C/G                        G
    Little something against the wind.

    C/G       Bm        Am          C/G     G
    I found myself ___ seeking shelter against ___ the wind.
    |         |         |           |       |
```

Piano Solo

```
| G        |     | Bm     |       |
| C/G  | G     | D      | C/G   |
| G        |     | Bm     |       |
| C/G  | G     | C/G    | D     |
```

Pre-Chorus 3

```
              Em        D         G
Well, those drifter's days __ are past me now,

              Em          C/G        G
I've got so ___ much more to think about.

Em      D            C/G
    Dead-lines and com-mitments,

                    D
What to leave in,    what to leave out.
```

Chorus 3

```
G                 Bm
    Against the wind,

C/G                        G
    I'm still runnin' against the wind.

    C/G     Bm        Am          C/G     G
    I'm older now ___ but still runnin' against ___ the wind.

              C/G     Bm        D              C/G
Well, I'm old - er now ___ and still runnin' against the wind.
```

Outro

```
                  G                 C/G
‖: Against the wind.  (Against the wind.)

                        G
I'm still runnin'. ( Against the wind.)   :‖  Repeat and fade
                                              (w/voc. ad lib.)
```

American Storm

Words and Music by
Bob Seger

Head-in' out on some un - chart-ed path, _

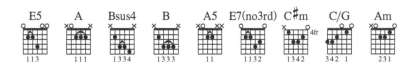

E5   A   Bsus4   B   A5   E7(no3rd)   C#m   C/G   Am

Intro

‖: E5 | | A | Bsus4 B :‖
| E5 | | | |

Verse 1

E5   A5
Headin' out on some uncharted path, you soon turn back

Bsus4   B   E5
It happens time ____ and time again,

                    A5   Bsus4 B
You never seem to reach the end.

E5
Someone's out there on the street tonight,

        A5   Bsus4   B   E5
When things go wrong he'll guarantee ____ to make them right

        A5   Bsus4 B
If the price is right.

Pre-Chorus 1

        A
Ev'ry time I look you're fallin', fallin'

E5   E7(no 3rd)
Beaten by the wind.

A   Bsus4 B
Ev'ry time I turn around he's there a - gain.

Chorus 1

        E5   **C♯m**

It's like a full force gale, an American storm.

                 A

You're buried far beneath a mountain of cold

            Bsus4

And you never get warm.

B   **E5**   **C♯m**

It's like a wall of mirrors, you charge 'em at full speed,

                A   **Bsus4**

You cover up, you hear the shattering glass but you never bleed,

B   **E5**   **A Bsus4 B E5 A Bsus4 B**

You never feel the need.

Verse 2

E5   **A5**

Ev'rybody casts a certain light, a special gift,

   Bsus4   **B**   **E5**

It's theirs to use ____ for wrong or right

        A5   **Bsus4 B**

When you face the night.

E5

More and more we choose the easy way,

   A5   **Bsus4**   **B**   **E5**

We take no risks, we figure out ____ which games ____ to play

        A5   **Bsus4 B**

And how to make 'em pay.

Pre-Chorus 2

   A

Suddenly the pressure's fallin', fallin'

E5   **E7(no 3rd)**

Skies have all turned grey.

A   **Bsus4 B**

Suddenly the storm is heading straight your way.

Chorus 2

                E5   C#m
It's like a full force gale atop a mountain of cold.

                     A   Bsus4
You tell your story a - gain and again and it never gets old.

B   E5   C#m
   You face a wall of mirrors, you charge 'em at full speed,

                       A   Bsus4
You cover up, you hear the shattering glass but you never bleed.

B   E5   C#m
   You face a full force gale, an American storm

                     A
You're buried far beneath a mountain of cold

               Bsus4
And you never get warm.

               B
No you never get warm.

            E5   C#m
You face a wall of mirrors, you charge 'em at full speed,

                     A   Bsus4
You cover up, you hear the shattering glass but you never bleed.

B   C/G Am   E5   A Bsus4 B
   You never feel the need,   you never feel the need.

        E5   A Bsus4   B   E5   A
Never feel the need.   Nev - er feel the need.

Bsus4   B   E5   A Bsus4 B
   You never feel the need.

Outro   ‖: E5 | |A |Bsus4 B :‖ *Repeat and fade*
                                                            w/ vocal ad lib.

Beautiful Loser

Words and Music by
Bob Seger

Melody:

He wants to dream like a young man

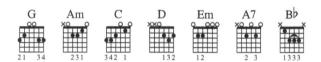

G   Am   C   D   Em   A7   B♭

Intro

| G | | |

Verse 1

G   Am
He wants to dream like a young man

C   D
With the wisdom of an old man.

G   Am
He wants his home and security,

C   D
He wants to live like a sailor at sea.

Chorus 1

Em   C   D Em   A7
Beautiful loser,   where you gonna fall

                G   Am D
When you realize you just can't have it all?

Verse 2

G   Am
He's your oldest and your best friend,

C   D
If you need him he'll be there again.

G   Am
He's always willing to be second best;

C   D
A perfect lodger, a perfect guest.

Chorus 2

```
Em        C   D Em              A7
   Beautiful loser,      read it on the wall

   G                           Am
And realize you just can't have it all.

D              Bb
Just can't have it all.
```

Bridge

```
C                 G
   You just can't have it all.

Bb C              G
Oh, oh, oh, can't have it all, ___ oh.

Bb C                              G
    You can try, you can try but you can't ___ have it all, whoa.

Bb C G       Bb              C                G
    Ah, yeah.   He'll never make any enemies, enemies, ___ no.

Bb              C            G
   He won't complain if he's caught in a freeze.

Bb              C
   He'll always ask, he'll always say please.
```

Piano Solo

```
|G      |Am      |C      |D      |
|G      |Am      |C      |D      |
```

Chorus 3

```
Em        C   D Em              A7
   Beautiful loser,      never take it all

   G                           Am
'Cause it's easier and faster when you fall

   D              C Em
You just don't need it all,

Am      D
   Oh, you just don't need it all.
```

Outro

```
|G      |      |      |Am      |

C D
   You just don't need it all.

||: G      |Am      |C      |D      :||   Repeat and fade
                                          w/ vocal ad lib.
```

Betty Lou's Gettin' Out Tonight

Words and Music by
Bob Seger

Melody:

Have you heard the news? _

Intro

F				
Bb7		F		
C		F		

Verse 1

F
Have you heard the news? It's all over town.

If you ain't heard it, boys, you better sit down.

Bb7
I got the story here, it's hot off the press.

F
Brace yourself, now, take a deep breath.

C
Grab a hold of somethin', hold on tight.

F
Betty Lou's gettin' out tonight.

Verse 2

    F

First heard the rumor down on Twelfth and Main.

The poor druggist, he was goin' insane.

B♭7

His stuff is sellin' out like never before.

F

He fin'lly had to up and close the store.

C

All the boys are gettin' ready to fight.

F

Betty Lou's gettin' out tonight.

Chorus 1

    F

Betty Lou's gettin' out tonight.

Betty Lou's gettin' out tonight.

B♭7

She was bad. Her mama got mad,

F

But now her mama says it's all right.

C

All the boys are gettin' ready and right.

F

Betty Lou's gettin' out tonight.

Interlude 1

F N.C.   **F N.C.**

   Betty Lou,   Betty Lou.

B♭7 N.C.   **F N.C.**

   It's all true.   It's really true.

C   **F**

Shouted: What do you think about that, boys? Yeah!

Guitar Solo   *Repeat Intro*

Saxophone Solo   *Repeat Intro*

Interlude 2	**F** N.C. **F** N.C.
	   Betty Lou, Betty Lou.
	
	Bb7 N.C. **F** N.C.
	    Yes, it's true. Betty Lou.
	
	C **F**
	   Uh, uh.

Outro-Chorus	**F**
	Well, ___ Betty Lou's gettin' out tonight.
	
	Betty Lou's gettin' out tonight.
	
	Bb7
	   She was bad. Her mama got mad,
	
	F
	   But now her mama says it's all right.
	
	C
	   All the boys are gettin' ready and right.
	
	F
	   Betty Lou's gettin' out tonight.
	
	C
	   Her mama said that it would be all right.
	
	F
	   Betty Lou's gettin' out tonight.
	
	C
	   Grab a hold of somethin', hold on tight.
	
	F
	   Betty Lou's gettin' out tonight.

Brand New Morning

Words and Music by
Bob Seger

Melody:

It's a brand new   morn - ing __

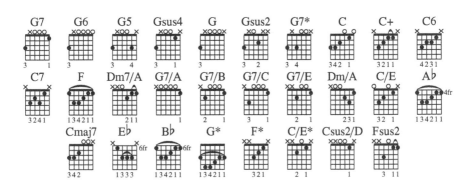

Intro |**4/4** G7 G6 G5 Gsus4 |G Gsus2 G G7* |**2/4** C |

| G7   C
Verse 1   It's a brand new morning

        C+   C6
        Of a brand new day.

        C7   F
        It's brand new chance

                         Dm7/A   G7 G7/A
        To make it all ____ work out some way.

        G7/B G7/C G7/B G7/E   Dm/A   Dm7/A   G7
        Right the wrongs ____ within the songs ____ of yesterday.

Verse 2

          N.C.   C
And, hey! Get a brand new feelin'

C+   C6
Get a brand new smile.

C7   F
Do some brand new things

                     Dm7/A   G7 G7/A
You just might see ____ after a while.

G7/B G7/C G7/B G7/E Dm/A   Dm7/A   G7 G7/A
          That   your   life takes on a shin - y, brand new star.

| G7/B G7/C G7/B G7/E |F   C/E |C7 |

Bridge 1

F   A♭   C Cmaj7 C Cmaj7
   Forget the past you know that's ancient history.

C Cmaj7 C Cmaj7 A♭
           It's a   time to be reborn,

                     E♭
It's a time for being free.

                   B♭   E♭   B♭
Someone might be wait - in', get outside ____ where you can see

E♭   B♭ E♭   G*
And you just might see,   yeah, you just might see

Verse 3

N.C.   C
  That it's a brand new morning

C+   C6
With a brand new sun

C7   F   Dm7/A   G7 G7/A
And it's just as warm for you as it is for ev'ry one.

G7/B G7/C G7/B G7/E Dm/A
           Don't just   walk,

                   Dm7/A   G7 G7/A
Come on get it on, ____ get on the run.

G7/B G7/C G7/B G7/E F
      It's a brand new   morning,

G7   F* C/E* Csus2/D
Mmm, it's a brand new day,

F* C/E* Csus2/D F* C/E* Csus2/D
             Yeah.

| G7 G6 G5 Gsus4 |G Gsus2 G G7* |

Instrumental | C | C+ | C6 | C7 |
                | F | Dm7/A | G7 G7/A | G7/B G7/C G7/B G7/E |
                | Dm/A | Dm7/A | G7 G7/A | G7/B G7/C G7/B G7/E |
                | Fsus2 C/E* | C7 |

Bridge 2   *Repeat Bridge 1*

Verse 4
N.C.   C
  That it's a brand new morning

C+   C6
  With a brand new sun

C7   F   Dm7/A   G7 G7/A
  And it's just as warm for you as it is for ev'ry one.

G7/B G7/C G7/B G7/E Dm/A
     Don't just   walk,

                   Dm7/A   G7 G7/A
Come on get it on, ___ get on the run.

G7/B G7/C G7/B G7/E F
     It's a brand new   morning,

G7   F* C/E* Csus2/D
Ooh, it's a brand new day,

F* C/E* Csus2/D F* C/E* Csus2/D
                   Yeah.

| G7 G6 G5 Gsus4 | G Gsus2 G G7* | C   G7   ‖

By the River

Words and Music by
Bob Seger

Melody:

I was walk - in'

(Capo 1st fret)

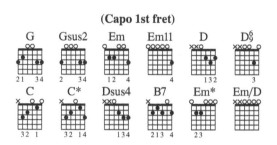

G   Gsus2   Em   Em11   D   D§

C   C*   Dsus4   B7   Em*   Em/D

Intro

| G   Gsus2 | G   Gsus2 | Em Em11 | Em   Em11 |
| D   D§ | D | C   C* | Dsus4 N.C. |

Verse 1

       G   Gsus2 G Gsus2 Em Em11
I was walkin'   by the river.

Em Em11 D   D§ D   C
   I held my hand out   to feel the rain.

Dsus4 D   G   Gsus2 G Gsus2 Em   Em11
   Just a light rain,   al - most a sun shower

Em Em11 D   D§ D   C*
   Makin' all things   shine ___ again.

             D   G
And I felt like I belonged,

  B7 Em*   Em/D C
I felt so strong as I walked on.

Verse 2

              G   **Gsus2 G Gsus2**   **Em Em11**
There was rhythm,   there was order.

Em   **Em11 D**   **D§** **D**   **C**
 There was a balance,   there was a flow.

Dsus4 D   **G**   **Gsus2 G Gsus2 Em**   **Em11**
    There was patience,   in - dulgence.

Em   **Em11 D**   **D§** **D**   **C**
 There was a power   I could not know.

               D   **G**
And I felt it all ___ made sense,

B7   **Em*** **Em/D**   **C**
Innocence, ___ a permanence.

Instrumental   *Repeat Verse 2*

Outro

          G   **Gsus2 G Gsus2 Em Em11**
I took my young son   to the river.

Em Em11   **D**   **D§** **D**   **C***
 I held his hand out   to feel the rain.

| **G** **Gsus2** | **G** **Gsus2** | **G** **Gsus2** | **G**   ‖

Chances Are

Words and Music by
Bob Seger

Chanc-es are ___ you'll find ___ me some - where on ___

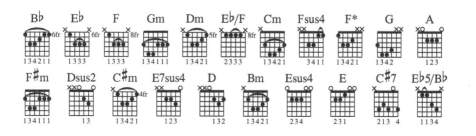

Intro

| Bb | Eb F | Bb | Eb F | |

Verse 1

        Bb   **Gm**
Male: Chances are you'll find ___ me

             Eb   **Bb**
Somewhere on ___ your road tonight.

              Gm   **Dm Eb Eb/F**
Seems I always end ___ up drivin' by.

Bb   **Gm**
Ever since I've known ___ you,

        Eb   **Bb**
It just seems ___ you're on my way,

           Gm   **Dm Eb**
All the rules of log - ic don't apply.

Pre-Chorus 1

             Cm   **Bb**
I long to see ___ you in the night,

Eb   **Cm**   **Fsus4 F* G**
Be with you ___ till morning light.

Verse 2

          A   F#m
Female: I remember clear - ly

      Dsus2   **A**
How you looked the night we met.

         F#m   **C#m Dsus2 E7sus4**
I recall your laugh - ter and your smile.

A   **F#m**   **Dsus2**   **A**
I remember how ____ you made me feel so at ease.

         F#m   **C#m**   **Dsus2**
I remember all ____ your grace, your style.

Pre-Chorus 2

D   **Bm**   **A**
  And now you're all ____ I long to see.

D   **Bm**   **Esus4 E**
  You've come to mean ____ so much to me.

Chorus 1

     A   **F#m**   **D**   **A**
Both: Chances are I'll see ____ you somewhere in my dreams tonight.

        F#m   **C#m Dsus2 E7sus4**
You'll be smilin' like ____ the night we met.

A   **F#m**   **D**   **A**
Chances are I'll hold ____ you and I'll of - fer all I have.

D   **C#m**   **Bm**   **A**   **E**
You're the on - ly one ____ I can't ____ forget.

   D   **A**
Male: Baby, you're the best I've ever met.

Bridge

       C#7   F#m

Both: And I'll be dreamin' of the fu - ture,

C#7   F#m

And hopin' you'll be by my side.

    Bm   A

Male: And in the morning I'll be long - ing

    D   A E   C#m Bm F#m E F*

Both: For the night, for the night.

Chorus 2

    Bb   Gm   Eb   Bb

Both: Chances are I'll see ___ you somewhere in my dreams tonight.

           Gm   Dm   Eb F

You'll be smilin' like ___ the night we met.   *Female:* Oh.

    Bb   Gm   Eb   Bb

Both: Chances are I'll hold ___ you and I'll of - fer all I have.

Eb   Dm   Cm   Bb   F

You're the on - ly one ___ I can't ___ forget.

Eb5/Bb

Baby, you're the best I've ever met.

Outro

    Bb Eb Eb/F Bb

Male: Oo, hoo.

     Eb F Bb

Female: Oo, hoo.

Even Now

Words and Music by
Bob Seger

Melody:

There's a high - way,

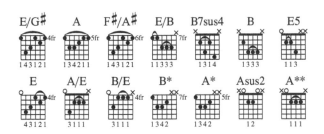

Intro

```
‖: E/G♯    |A      |F♯/A♯   |        :‖
|E/G♯     |A      |F♯/A♯   |        |
|E/B      |       |B7sus4  B |      |
|E5       |       |        |        |
```

Verse 1

    E   A/E   B/E   A/E   E
There's a highway, a lonesome stretch of gray.

           A/E   B/E   A/E E
It runs be - tween us and takes me far away.

         A/E   B/E   A/E   E
Out in the distance, always with - in reach,

         A/E   B/E   A/E   E5
There's a crossroad where all the vic - tims meet.

Pre-Chorus 1

     A   E/G♯
I close my eyes and see her face,

    B*   A*   E5
It's all I want to see.

     A   E/G♯   B
And deep inside it still amazes me.

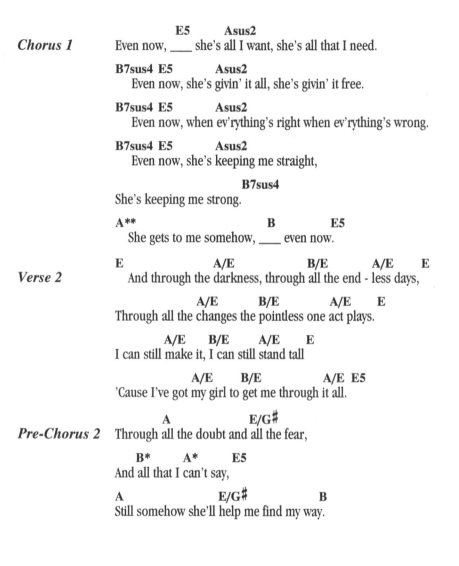

Chorus 1

          E5   Asus2
Even now, ___ she's all I want, she's all that I need.

B7sus4 E5   Asus2
  Even now, she's givin' it all, she's givin' it free.

B7sus4 E5   Asus2
  Even now, when ev'rything's right when ev'rything's wrong.

B7sus4 E5   Asus2
  Even now, she's keeping me straight,

                    B7sus4
She's keeping me strong.

A**   B   E5
  She gets to me somehow, ___ even now.

Verse 2

E   A/E   B/E   A/E   E
  And through the darkness, through all the end - less days,

       A/E   B/E   A/E   E
Through all the changes the pointless one act plays.

      A/E   B/E   A/E   E
I can still make it, I can still stand tall

        A/E   B/E   A/E E5
'Cause I've got my girl to get me through it all.

Pre-Chorus 2

         A   E/G#
Through all the doubt and all the fear,

     B*   A*   E5
And all that I can't say,

A   E/G#   B
Still somehow she'll help me find my way.

Chorus 2

        E5   **Asus2**
Even now, ___ she's still in my heart, she's still in my soul.

B7sus4 E5   **Asus2**
Even now, she's still on my mind wherever I go.

B7sus4 E5   **Asus2**
Even now, through all of my days and all of my nights.

B7sus4 E5   **Asus2**   **B7sus4**
Even now, she's keeping it real, she's keeping it right.

A**   **B**   **E5**
She gets to me somehow, ___ even now.

Interlude

| E   A/E | | B/E   A/E | E |
Even

| A/E | | B/E   A/E | E |
Now.   Oh, even now.

| A/E | | B/E   A/E | E |
Even

| A/E | | B/E   A/E | E5 |
Now.   Oh.

Outro-Chorus

E A/E   B/E   A/E   E
(She's all that I want, she's all that I need.)

        A/E   B/E   A/E   E
Even now. ___ (She's givin' it all, she's givin' it free.)

     A/E   B/E   A/E   E
Oh. ___ (When ev'rything's right when ev'rything's wrong.)

     A/E   B/E
Oh.   (She's keeping it real, she's keeping it strong.)

A** **B** **A**** **B**   **E5**
Oh, oh.   Even now.

Face the Promise

Words and Music by
Bob Seger

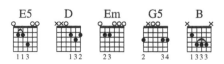

Intro   ‖: **E5** | | | :‖

Verse 1
              E5
I've been down ___ in the Delta, workin' these fields.

Breakin' my back, I need a better deal.

So long Mississippi, so long Alabam'.

I wanna face the promise of the promised land.

Verse 2
          E5
I've got fevered dreams, mighty plans.

I need a blacktop road, I need a wheel in my hands.

So long Arizona, so long desert sands.

I need to face the promise of the promised land.

Verse 3

E5

I'm tired ____ of this river and these nothin' nights.

I'm small-towned out, I need city lights.

So long, Allegheny, so long, Olean.

I need to face the promise of the promised land.

Bridge

D   **Em**

I need a world of changes,   I need a brand new space.

D   **G5**   **B**

I need an El Dorado,   there's got to be some place.

Guitar Solo

‖: **E5** | | | :‖

Verse 4

E5

There's a line inside I think I've crossed.

You better watch out now, I'm gonna be my own boss.

So long, Massachusetts, so long, Framingham.

I need to face the promise of the promised land.

So long, North Dakota, you must understand

I need to face the promise of the promised land.

Guitar Solo

‖: **E5** | | | :‖ *Play 4 times*

(Face the promise.)

The Fire Down Below

Words and Music by
Bob Seger

Here comes _old_ Ros - ie,

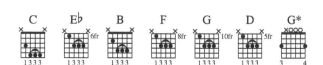

Intro | C | E♭ C | | E♭ C |
         | | | | B |

Verse 1

    C

Here comes old Rosie, she's looking mighty fine;

Here comes hot Nancy, she's steppin' right on time.

There go the street lights, bringing on the night;

Here come the men, faces hidden from the light.

F   E♭   C

All through the shadows,   oh, they come and they go,

              G   F   C

With only one ___ thing in common,   they got the fire down below.

                         C
Verse 2   Here comes the rich man in his big long limousine;

             Here comes the poor man, all you got to have is green.

             Here comes the banker, and the lawyer and the cop;

             One thing for certain, it ain't never gonna stop.
             F   Eb   C
                When it all gets too heavy,   that's when they come and they go, __ they go,
                      G   F   C
             With only one ___ thing in common,   they got the fire down below.

                     F   C
Bridge   Yeah, it happens out in Vegas and it happens in Moline,

                    F
             On the blue - blood streets of Boston,

                    C
             Up in Berke - ley and out in Queens.

                  F   C
             And it went on yesterday and it's going on tonight.

                  D   G*
             Some - where there's somebody ain't treatin' ___ somebody right.

                     C
Verse 3   And he's a looking out for Rosie, she's looking mighty fine;

             And he's walking the streets for Nancy, and he'll find her ev'rytime.

                      B   C
             And when the   streetlights flicker, bringing on the night,

             Well, they'll be slipping into darkness, slipping out of sight.
             F   Eb   C
                All through the midnight,   watch 'em come and watch 'em go, oh, go.
                      G   F   C
             With only one ___ thing in common,   they got the fire down below.

             Oh, burning down below.

Guitar Solos   *Repeat Verse 1 (Instrumental)*

                           F   C

Bridge 2   Yeah, it happens out in Vegas, happens in Moline,

                            F

On the blue - blood streets of Boston,

                       E♭   D   C

Up in Berke - ley and out in Queens.

                     F   C

And it went on yesterday and it's going on tonight.

                    D   G*

Some - where there's somebody ain't treatin' ____ somebody right.

                     C

Verse 4   And he's a looking out for Rosie, she's looking mighty fine;

And he's walking the streets for Nancy, and he'll find her ev'rytime.

And when the streetlights flicker, bringing on the night,

Well, they'll be slipping into darkness, slipping out of sight.

F

  All through the shadows,

E♭   C

  Watch 'em come and watch 'em go, oh, they go.

                 G   F   C

With only one ____ thing in common,   they got the fire down below.

                 G   F   C

Oh, they got one ____ thing in common,   they got the fire down below.

                 G   F N.C.

Only got one ____ thing in common   they got the fire down below.

C

  One, two, three…

Outro-
Guitar Solo ‖: C | | | :‖

Get Out of Denver

Words and Music by
Bob Seger

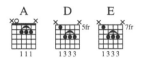

A   *D*   *E*

Intro | A | |

Verse 1

    A

I still remember it was autumn and the moon was shinin',

                            D

Our '60 Cadillac was roarin' through Nebraska, whin - in'.

                            A

Doin' a hundred-twenty, man, the fields was bendin' o - ver;

                            E

Headin' out for the mountains, knowin' we was travelin' fur - ther.

                            A

All the fires were blazin' and the spinnin' wheels were turnin', turn - in';

Had my girl beside me, brother, brother, she was burnin', burnin'.

Guitar Solo   *Repeat Verse 1 (Instrumental)*

Verse 2

    A

Up walked a Baptist-preachin', southern, funky schoolteacher,

                            D

She had a line on somethin' heavy but we couldn't reach her.

                            A

We told her that we needed somethin' that would get us go - in';

                            E

She pulled out all she had and laid it on the counter, show - in'!

All I had to do was lay my money down and pick it up;

    A

Cops came bustin' in and then we lit out in a pickup truck.

Chorus 1	**A** Go. Get out of Denver, better go, go.

A
Chorus 1   Go. Get out of Denver, better go, go.

        D
Get out of Denver, better go.

       A
Get out of Denver, better go, go.

         E
Get out of Denver, 'cause you look just like a commie

And you might just be a member.

    A
Better get out of Denver, better get out of Denver.

    D
Bridge   Well, ____ red lights were flashin' and the sirens were a screamin';

A   **D**
 We had to pinch each other just to see if we was dream - in'?

Made it to Loveland Pass in under less than half an hour;

E
Lord, it started drizzlin' and it turned into a thunder shower.

Guitar Solo 2 ||: A | | | |
         | D | | A | |
         | E | | A | :||

Organ Solo *Repeat Guitar Solo 2*

Verse 3

A

The rain kept drivin' but the Caddy kept on burnin rubber;

D

We kept on drivin' till we ran into some fog cov - er.

E

We couldn't see a thing, somehow we just kept on go - in';

E

We kept on drivin' all night long and then into the morn - in' fog.

It finally lifted when we looked to see where we was at,

A

We were starin' at a Colorado state policeman trooper cat and...

Chorus 2

A

Go. Get out of Denver, he said go, go.

D

Get out of Denver, better go.

A

Get out of Denver, better go, go.

E

Get out of Denver, 'cause you look just like a commie

And you might just be a member.

A

Better   get out of Denver, better get out of Denver.

Outro-Chorus

A

Better go! Oh, better, better, better go!

D   A

Hey, go. Ah, better, better go! Go, go, go!

E

'Cause you look just like a commie and you might just be a member.

A   N.C.   A

Better   get out of Denver, better go!

The Fire Inside

Words and Music by
Bob Seger

Melody:

There's a   hard moon   ris - in'

(Capo 4th fret)

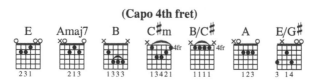

E   Amaj7   B   C#m   B/C#   A   E/G#

Intro   ‖: E | | Amaj7 | :‖

Verse 1

        E
There's a hard moon risin' on the streets tonight,

        Amaj7   E   Amaj7
There's a reckless feeling in your heart as you head out tonight.

        E
Through the concrete canyons to the midtown lights,

        Amaj7   E   Amaj7
Where the latest neon promises are burning bright.

        E
Past the open windows on the darker streets,

        Amaj7   E   Amaj7
Where un - seen angry voices flash and children cry.

        E
Past the phony posers with their worn out lines,

      Amaj7
The tired new money dressed to the nines,

      E
The lowlife dealers with their bad designs

      Amaj7
And the dilettantes with their open minds.

Pre-Chorus 1

B
You're out on the town, safe in the crowd,

C#m   B/C# C#m
Ready to go for the ride.

A
Searching the eyes, looking for clues,

E/G#   B
There's no way you can hide.

E Amaj7   E   Amaj7
Chorus 1   The fire in - side.

            E
Verse 2   Well you've been to the clubs and the discotheques,

        Amaj7
Where they deal one another

                        E   Amaj7
From the bottom of a deck of promises.

        E
Where the cautious loners and emotional wrecks

        Amaj7   E   Amaj7
Do an acting stretch as a way to hide the obvious.

        E
And the lights go down and they dance real close,

        Amaj7   E   Amaj7
And for one brief instant they pretend they're safe and warm.

        E
Then the beat gets louder and the mood is gone,

        Amaj7
The darkness scatters as the lights flash on.

        E
They hold one another just a little too long

        Amaj7
And they move apart and then move on.

Pre-Chorus 2

B
On to the street, on to the next,

C#m   B/C# C#m
Safe in the knowledge that they tried.

A
Faking the smile, hiding the pain,

E/G#   B
Never satisfied.

Chorus 2

E Amaj7   E Amaj7   E Amaj7
    The fire in - side.   Fire in - side.

Piano Solo

‖: E | |Amaj7 | :‖ *Play 9 times*

Verse 3

           E
Now, the hour is late and he thinks you're asleep.

    Amaj7
You listen to him dress and you listen to him leave

      E   Amaj7
Like you knew he would.

      E
You hear his car pull away in the street,

    Amaj7
Then you move to the door and you lock it

      E   Amaj7
When he's gone for good.

      E
Then you walk to the window and stare at the moon

Amaj7   E   Amaj7
Riding high and lonesome through a star - lit sky.

     E
And it comes to you how it all slips away,

Amaj7
Youth and beauty are gone one day.

     E
No matter what you dream or feel or say,

   Amaj7
It ends in dust and disarray.

Pre-Chorus 3

B
Like wind on the plains, sand through the glass,

C#m   **B/C#** **C#m**
Waves rolling in with the tide.

A
Dreams die hard and we watch them erode

     E/G#   **B**
But we cannot be denied.

Chorus 3

E Amaj7   **E** **Amaj7** **E**
   The fire in - side.   Fire in - side.

Amaj7   **E** **Amaj7**   **E**
  Oh, fire in - side.   Burning you up.

           Amaj7   **E** **Amaj7**
Burning you up. Fire in - side.

Outro-Piano Solo   ‖: E | |Amaj7 | :‖ *Repeat and fade*

Fire Lake

Words and Music by
Bob Seger

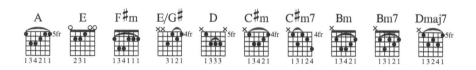

Who's gon-na ride ___ that chrome three ___ wheel - er?

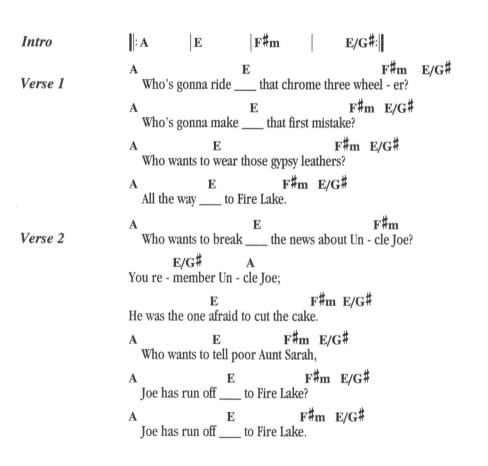

A	E	F#m	E/G#	D	C#m	C#m7	Bm	Bm7	Dmaj7

Intro   ‖: A |E |F#m | E/G#:‖

Verse 1

    A   E   F#m E/G#
Who's gonna ride ___ that chrome three wheel - er?

    A   E   F#m E/G#
Who's gonna make ___ that first mistake?

    A   E   F#m E/G#
Who wants to wear those gypsy leathers?

    A   E   F#m E/G#
All the way ___ to Fire Lake.

Verse 2

    A   E   F#m
Who wants to break ___ the news about Un - cle Joe?

      E/G#   A
You re - member Un - cle Joe;

           E   F#m E/G#
He was the one afraid to cut the cake.

    A   E   F#m E/G#
Who wants to tell poor Aunt Sarah,

    A   E   F#m E/G#
Joe has run off ___ to Fire Lake?

    A   E   F#m E/G#
Joe has run off ___ to Fire Lake.

Interlude

     D   **C♯m**   **F♯m**
Who wants to brave those bronze beauties   lying in the sun,

           C♯m   **C♯m7** **Bm**
With their long soft hair fall - ing,   flyin' as they run?

Bm7   **D**   **Dmaj7**
Oh, they smile so shy and they flirt ___ so well

        A
And they lay you down so fast.

        E
Till you look straight up and say, "Oh Lord, am I really here at last?"

Verse 3

A   **E**   **F♯m** **E/G♯**
Who wants to play those eights and aces?

A   **E**   **F♯m** **E/G♯**
Who want a raise, who needs a stake?

A   **E**   **F♯m**   **E/G♯**
Who wants to take that long shot gamble, ha,

A   **E**   **F♯m**
And head out ___ to Fire Lake?

Outro

    E/G♯   **A**   **E**   **F♯m**
‖: And head out. __ (Who wants to go to Fire Lake?)   :‖ *Repeat and*
                                                        fade w/ lead
                                                        vocal ad lib.

Her Strut

Words and Music by
Bob Seger

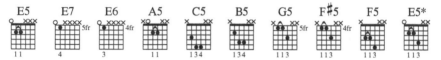

She's to - tal - ly ___ com-mit - ted

Tune down 1/2 step:
(low to high) Eb -Ab -Db -Gb -Bb -Eb

E5 E7 E6 A5 C5 B5 G5 F#5 F5 E5*

Intro

| E5 | | | | |
|:E5 | E7 | E6 E7 | E5 :|

Verse 1

       E5   E7
She's totally committed to major independence,

       E6   E7   E5
But she's a lady through and ___ through.

                            E7
She gives them quite a battle, all ___ that they can handle;

       E6   E7   E5
She'll bruise some, she'll hurt some, ___ too.

Chorus 1

       A5 C5   E5
But oh,   they love to watch her strut.

A5 C5   B5
Oh,   they do respect her but

          N.C.   E5
They love ___ to watch her strut. Uh!

E7   E6 E7 E5   E7 E6 E7 E5
  Oh, yeah.   Oh.

Verse 2

    E5   E7
Some - times they'll want to leave her, just give up and leave her,

    E6   E7   E5
But they would never play that scene.

                    E7
In spite of all her talking, once she starts in walking,

    E6   E7   E5
The lady will be all they ever dreamed.

Chorus 2

    A5 C5   E5
But oh,   they'll love to watch her strut.

    A5 C5   B5
Oh,   they'll kill to make the cut,

           N.C.   E5
They love ____ to watch her strut.

    E7   E6 E7 E5   E7 E6 E7
  Oh, yeah.   Love to watch her.

    E5
  Watch her strut, now.

Guitar Solo   ‖: E5 |E7 |E6   E7|E5   :‖

Chorus 3

    A5 C5   E5   G5 F#5 F5 E5*
Oh,   they love to watch her   strut.

    A5 C5   B5
Oh,   they do respect her but

          N.C.   E5
They love ____ to watch her strut. Mm!

    E7   E6 E7 E5
  Alright.   *Ah.* Love her strut.

    E7   E6   E7   E5
  Mm, hmm.   *Love to, love ____ to,*   love to watch her strut.

Outro   ‖: E5 |E7 |E6   E7|E5   :‖ *Repeat and fade*
                                                               w/ vocal ad lib.

Hollywood Nights

Words and Music by
Bob Seger

Melody:

She stood there bright as the sun on that

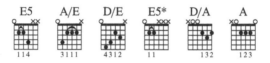

E5   A/E   D/E   E5*   D/A   A

Intro

‖: E5 | |A/E | |
|D/E | |E5 | :‖

Verse 1

E5*
   She stood there bright as the sun on that California coast.
                                                      A/E

D/E   E5*
   He was a Midwestern boy on his own.

                                         A/E
She looked at him with those soft eyes, so innocent and blue.

D/E   E5*
   He knew right then he was too far from home.

Interlude 1

E5   A/E   D/E   E5
   Oo,   he was too far from home.

Verse 2

E5*   A/E
She took his hand and she led him along ___ that golden beach.

D/E   E5*
They watched the waves tumble over the sand.

                                    A/E
They drove for miles and miles up those twisting, turning roads.

D/E   E5*
Higher and higher and higher they climbed.

Chorus 1

              E5   A/E
And those Hol - lywood nights in those Hol - lywood hills.

           D/E   E5
She was look - ing so right in her dia - monds and frills.

                     A/E
All those big city nights in those high, ___ rolling hills;

      D/E   E5
A - bove all the lights, she had all ___ of the skills.

Bridge

D/A			A		
		Ah.		Yeah!	

E5		A/E	E5		
				Ow.	

		Mm.		

Verse 3

E5*   A/E
He'd headed west 'cause he felt that a change would do him good.

D/E   E5*
See some old friends; good for the soul.

                                A/E
She had been born with a face that would let her get her way.

D/E   E5*
He saw that face and he lost all con - trol.

| | E5   A/E   D/E   E5 |
| *Interlude 2* | Yeah,   he had lost all control. |

| *Verse 4* | E5*   A/E |
| | Night after night and day after day, ___ it went on and on. |

D/E   E5*
Then came that morning he woke up a - lone.

                                    A/E
He spent all night staring down at the lights of L.A.,

D/E   E5*
Wondering if he could ever go home.

| *Chorus 2* | E5   A/E |
| | And those Hol - lywood nights in those Hol - lywood hills. |

D/E   E5
It was look - ing so right, it was giv - ing him chills.

                          A/E
In those big city nights, in those high, ___ rolling hills;

D/E   E5
A - bove all the lights, with a pas - sion that kills.

| *Chorus 3* | E5   A/E |
| | In those Hol - lywood nights in those Hol - lywood hills. |

D/E   E5
She was look - ing so right in her dia - monds and frills.

                          A/E
All those big city lights in those high, ___ rolling hills;

D/E   E5
A - bove all the lights, she had all ___ of the skills.

| *Outro* | E5   A/E |
| | ‖: (Hol - lywood nights. Hol - lywood hills. |

D/E   E5
A - bove all the lights. Hol - lywood nights.) :‖ *Repeat and*
                                                   fade w/ lead
                                                   vocal ad lib.

Like a Rock

Words and Music by
Bob Seger

Stood there bold - ly,   sweat-in' in the sun. ____

(Capo 1st fret)

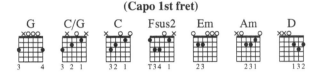

Intro | G   C/G | G | C/G | G |

Verse 1
G
Stood there boldly, sweatin' in the sun.

C
Felt like a million, felt like number one.

Fsus2   C
The height of summer, I'd never felt that strong,

    G   C/G G
Like a rock.

Verse 2
G
I was eighteen, didn't have a care.

C
Workin' for peanuts, not a dime to spare.

Fsus2   C
But I was lean and solid ev'rywhere,

    G   C/G G
Like a rock.

Verse 3
G
My hands were steady, my eyes were clear and bright.

C
My walk had purpose, my steps were quick and light.

Fsus2   C
And I held firmly, to what I felt was right,

    G   C/G G
Like a rock.

Chorus 1

      G
Like a rock, I was strong as I could be.

      C
Like a rock, nothin' ever got to me.

      Fsus2   **C**
Like a rock, I was somethin' to see.

      G   **C/G G**
Like a rock.

Bridge

      Em
And I stood arrow straight, unencumbered by the weight

      G
Of all these hustlers and their schemes.

      C
I stood proud, I stood tall, high above it all;

  Am   **D**
I still believed in my dreams.

Guitar Solo

```
‖: G        |          | C          |            |
 | Fsus2   | C        | G          |          :‖
 |        C/G | G    C/G | G   C/G | G    C/G |
```

Verse 4

G
   Twenty years now, where'd they go?

C
   Twenty years, I don't know.

Fsus2   **C**   **G**
   I sit and I wonder sometimes   where they've gone.

Verse 5

G
And sometimes late at night,

C
Oh, when I'm bathed in the firelight,

Fsus2   C
The moon comes callin', a ghostly white,

       G
And I re - call, I recall.

Chorus 2

       G
Like a rock, standin' arrow straight.

      C
Like a rock, chargin' from the gate.

       Fsus2 C
Like a rock,   carryin' the weight.

       G
Like a rock.

Oh, like a rock, the sun upon my skin.

       C
Like a rock, hard against the wind.

       Fsus2   C
Like a rock, I see ___ myself again.

       G
Like a rock, oh, like a rock.

Outro-Guitar Solo

‖: G | | C | |
| Fsus2 | C | G | :‖ *Play 3 times*
| ‖

In Your Time

Words and Music by
Bob Seger

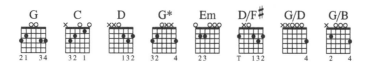

Intro

| G C | D | | C | G | |

Verse 1

    C   D   G*
In your time, the innocence will fall ___ away.

    C   D   Em
In your time the mission bells will toll.

        D   C   G*
Oh, all along ___ the corridors and riv - erbeds.

        C   D   C G*
There'll be sign ___ in your ___ time.

Verse 2

       C D   G
Tow'r - ing waves will crash across your south - ern capes.

         C D   Em
Massive ___ storms will reach your eastern shores.

        D   C   G
Fields of green ___ will tumble through your sum - mer days,

    C   D   C G*
By design ___ in your ___ time.

Bridge

      D/F#   **Em**   **G/D**   **C**

Feel the wind ____ and set yourself the bold - er course.

G* **D/F#**   **Em**   **G/D**   **C**

Keep your heart ____ as open as a shrine

          G/B   **D G C**

You'll sail ____ the perfect line.

Instrumental

D		G	C
D		Em	D
C		G	C
D		C	G*	

Verse 3

       C   **D**   **G***

After ____ all ____ the dead ends and the les - sons learned.

       C **D**   **Em**

After all ____ the stars have turned to stone.

        D   **C**   **G***

There'll be peace ____ across the great unbrok - en void.

    C   **D**   **C**   **G***

All benign ____ in your ____ time.

      C   **D**   **C**   **G***

You'll be fine ____ in your ____ time.

Katmandu

Words and Music
by Bob Seger

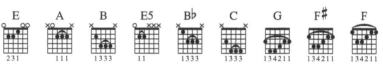

E   A   B   E5   B♭   C   G   F♯   F

Intro | N.C.(E) |

Chorus 1

N.C.(E)   A
I think I'm goin' to Kat - mandu,

                    E
That's really, really where I'm goin' to.

         B   E
If I ever get out ____ of here, that's what I'm gonna do.

      A   E
K-K-K-K-K-K- Katmandu, I think it's really where I'm goin' to.

         B
If I ever get out ____ of here, I'm goin' to Katmandu.

Verse 1

N.C.(E)   A
     I got no kick against the West Coast,

              E
Warner Brothers are such good hosts.

            B
I raise my whiskey glass and give 'em a toast,

           E
I'm sure they know it's true.

         A
I got no rap against the Southern states,

           E
Ev'ry time I've been there, it's been great.

         B
But now I'm leavin' and I can't be late,

         E
And to myself be true.

Chorus 2

    N.C.   A
That's why I'm goin' to Katmandu,

                        E
Up to the mountain's where I'm goin' to.

              B   E
Hey, if I ever get out ___ of here, that's what I'm gonna do.

                A   E
Ow! K-K-K-K-K- Kat - mandu, really, really where I'm goin' to.

              B
If I ever get out ___ of here, I'm goin' to Katmandu.

Verse 2

    N.C.(E)   A
    I got no quarrel with the Midwest,

                    E
The folks out there have given me their best.

                    B
I've lived there all my life, I've been their guest,

               E
I sure have loved it, too.

              A
I'm tired of lookin' at the TV news,

               E
I'm tired of drivin' hard and payin' dues.

            B
I figure, baby, I got nothin' to lose,

              E
I'm tired of being blue.

Chorus 3

    N.C.   A
Ow,   that's why I'm goin' to Katmandu,

                     E
Up to the mountain's where I'm goin' to.

              B   E
If I ever get out ___ of here, that's what I'm gonna do.

                A   E
Ow! K-K-K-K-K- Kat - mandu, take me, baby, 'cause I'm goin' with you.

             B   N.C.(E)
If I ever get out ___ of here, I'm goin' to Katmandu. ___ Oo!

| *Guitar Solo 1* | ‖: E5 | | | | :‖ |

Harmonica Solo	A		E		
	B		E		
	A		E		
	B				B♭

Saxophone Solo	A		E		
	A		N.C.(E)		

Verse 3

N.C.(E)   A
I ain't got nothin' 'gainst the East coast,

                     E
You want some people, well, they got the most.

                  B
And New York City's like a friendly ghost,

              E
You seem to pass right through.

          A
I know I'm gonna miss the U.S.A.,

           E
I guess I'll miss it ev'ry single day.

         B
But no one loves me here anyway,

        E
I know my plane is due.

Chorus 4

N.C.   A
The one that's goin' to Katmandu,

                          E
Up to the mountain's where I'm goin' to.

             B   E
If I ever get out ___ of here, that's what I'm gonna do.

               A   E
K-K-K-K-K-K- Kat - mandu, really, really, really goin' to.

             B
If I ever get out ___ of here, if I ever get out of here,

             C   B   N.C.(E)
If I ever get out ___ of here,   I'm going to Katmandu.

A   G
Ow! Oo, hu, hu.   Oo, hu, hu.

    F♯   F   E
Oo, ___ yeah, ___ yeah.

Outro-Guitar Solo ‖:
A   E
(Katmandu.   Katmandu.) :‖ *Repeat and fade*

Lock and Load

Words and Music by Bob Seger,
Craig Frost and Tim Mitchell

Tune down 1/2 step:
(low to high) Eb - Ab - Db - Gb - Bb - Eb

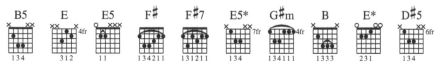

B5	E	E5	F#	F#7	E5*	G#m	B	E*	D#5

Intro

| B5 | E | B5 | E | |
| :B5 | E5 | B5 | E5 : |

Verse 1

           B5   E5
I wish I had a nickel for ev'ry time I fell

  B5   E5
And blamed somebody else.

  B5   E5
I'd give a ton of money to the ones I've hurt

   B5   E5
And I'd still be sittin' pretty well.

   B5   E
I've spent years losin' touch with what's right and what's real,

   B5   E
Caught up in these missions of my own.

    B5   E
And you're tellin' me you think I've done so damn well

   B5   E
While we're sittin' here a thousand miles from home.

Pre-Chorus 1
                          F
But there's a hole in your wisdom. A hole in your sky.

                       F#7
Two holes in your head where the light's supposed to get by.

Chorus 1
                       B5   E5*
    Time to lock and load.

                       B5   E5*
    Time to get control.

                       B5   E5*   B5 E5 B5
    Time to search the soul ___ and start again.

Verse 2
                       E5   B5   E5
    So many times I've seen chances disappear.

                        B5   E5
   I hesitate and watch them slip away.

                          B5   E5
   Like the time I fail to spend with the ones I love.

                          B5   E5
   And it's gone as sure as yesterday.

                          B5   E
   All these users and fakers, big-time takers,

                        B5   E
   Man - ipulating ev'ryone they see.

                        B5   E*
   I get caught up in their schemes and their use - less dreams.

                        B5   E*
   And the only one I have to blame is me.

	F#
Pre-Chorus 2	I get turned 'round and twisted, pulled left and right.

                                                  F#7
I can see where I'm goin' but I can't see the light.

Chorus 2

B5   E5*
  Time to lock and load.

B5   E5*
  Come in from the cold.

B5   E5*   B5 E5 B5
  Take a diff'rent road ___ and start again.

Bridge

E5   G#m   F#
  I can sit here in the back half of my life

    B   E*
And wonder when the other shoe will fall.

      G#m   E*
Or I can stand up, point myself home

    B   F#
And see if I've learned anything at all,

      D#5   E5*
Ahh, ___ anything at all.

B5   N.C. B5   N.C.
  Ooh,   ooh.

Guitar Solo   ‖: B5 | E5*   :‖ *Play 4 times*

Pre-Chorus 3
         F#
Medi - ocrity's easy. The good things take time.

         F#7
The great need commitment right down the line.

Chorus 3
  B5   E5*
  Time to lock and load.

  B5   E5*
  Come in from the cold.

  B5   E5*   B5 E5*
  Pay these debts I owe ___ and start again. ___   Ahh.

Chorus 4
  B5   E5*
  I've been down this road.

  B5   E5*
  I've seen things get old.

  B5   E5*   B5 E5*
  Time to get control ___ and start it all again.

Chorus 5
  B5   E5*
  Time to lock and load.

  B5   E5*
  Time to get control.

  B5   E5*   B5 E5*
  Time to search the soul ___ and start again.

Outro-Chorus
  B5   E5*
‖: I've been down this road.

  B5   E5*
  I've seen things get old.

  B5   E5   B5 E5*
  Stand up, get bold ___ and start again.   :‖ *Repeat*
                                            and fade

Lookin' Back

Words and Music by
Bob Seger

Melody:

They hit the street,

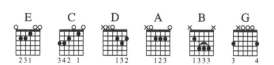

E   C   D   A   B   G

Intro   ‖: E | | | :‖

Verse 1
            E   **C**
They hit the street, you feel them starin'

              D   **A**   **E**
You know they hate you, you can feel their eyes a glarin'.

                        C
Because you're diff'rent, because you're free,

              D   **A**   **E**
Because you're ev'rything deep down they wish they could be.

Chorus 1
              E
You're lookin' back, (They lookin' back.)

      B
They lookin' back. (They lookin' back.)

A   **G**   **E**
Too many people lookin' back.

They lookin' back. (They lookin' back.)

      B
They lookin' back. (They lookin' back.)

A   **G**   **E**
Too many people lookin' back.

Verse 2

                        E   C
They watch the news, see young men dyin'.

                    D   A   E
They watch 'em bleedin' and they listen to them cryin'.

                            C
And if they're normal, if they can see

                    D   A   E
They just reach out and change the channel on the T - V.

Chorus 2

                      E
They lookin' back, (They lookin' back.)

                     B
They lookin' back. (They lookin' back.)

A   G   E
Too many people lookin' back.

They lookin' back. (They lookin' back.)

                     B
They lookin' back. (They lookin' back.)

A   G   E
Too many people lookin' back.

Interlude   ‖: E | | | :‖

Verse 3	**E** **C**

E   **C**
When they could vote, and end the war

         D   **A**   **E**
They're much too busy fittin' locks upon the back ___ door.

                  C
Give you a foxhole, a place to hide

            D   **A**   **E**
'Cause when the war ___ comes, the cops will be on their side, Lord.

Chorus 3   *Repeat Chorus 2*

Chorus 4

           E
They lookin' back, (They lookin' back.)

           B
They lookin' back. (They lookin' back.)

A   **G**   **E**
Too many people lookin' back.

They lookin' back. (They lookin' back.)

           B
They lookin' back. (They lookin' back.)

A **N.C.**   **A** **N.C.**
Too many people, too many people

A **N.C.**   **E**
Too many people lookin' back.

Old Time Rock & Roll

Melody:

Words and Music by
George Jackson and Thomas E. Jones III

Just take those old rec-ords off the shelf, —

(Capo 2nd fret)

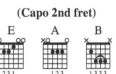

Intro

| N.C.(E) | N.C. | N.C.(E) | |

Verse 1

       N.C.   E
Just take those old records off the shelf,

                  A
I'll sit and listen to 'em by myself.

                  B
Today's music ain't got the same soul.

                E
I like that old time rock and roll.

Don't try to take me to a disco,

                  A
You'll never even get me out on the floor.

                B
In ten minutes I'll be late for the door.

                E
I like the old time rock and roll.

Chorus 1

      B   **E**
Still like that old time rock and roll,

                A
That kind of music just soothes the soul.

           B
I reminisce about the days of old

         E   **B**
With that old time rock and roll.

Guitar Solo

| E | | A | | |
| B | | E | | |

Verse 2

      B   **E**
Won't go to hear 'em play a Tango.

              A
I'd rather hear some blues or funky old soul.

              B
There's only one sure way to get me to go;

          E
Start playing old time rock and roll.

Call me a relic, call me what you will.

             A
Say I'm old fashioned, say I'm over the hill.

         B
Today's music ain't got the same soul.

         E
I like that old time rock and roll.

Chorus 2   *Repeat Chorus 1*

Sax Solo   *Repeat Guitar Solo*

Chorus 3	B E Still like that old time rock and roll,
	A That kind of music just soothes the soul.
	B I reminisce about the days of old
	E With that old time rock and roll.
Chorus 4	B N.C. Still like that old time rock and roll,
	That kind of music just soothes the soul.
	I reminisce about the days of old
	With that old time rock and roll.
Chorus 5	B E Still like that old time rock and roll,
	A That kind of music just soothes the soul.
	B I reminisce about the days of old
	E With that old time rock and roll.
	B Still like that old time rock and roll.
Outro-Guitar Solo	B E A B E B Still like that old time rock and roll.

‖: E | | A | |

| B | | E | B   :‖ *Repeat and fade*

Lucifer

Words and Music by
Bob Seger

Melody:

Cruis-in' on the grey snakes till my dy-in' day.

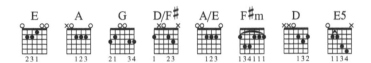

| E | A | G | D/F♯ | A/E | F♯m | D | E5 |

Intro |E | | |

Verse 1

E   A   G   D/F♯
Cruisin' on the grey snakes till my dyin' day.

A   G DF♯ A/E   E
Checkin' out the hen houses all along the way.

                A   G   D/F♯
Wastin' time and drinkin' wine,   life is short and I ___ ain't lyin'.

A   G   D/F♯   A
   Livin' all I can ___ through ev - 'ry day. ___ Yeah.

Chorus 1

A/E   E   F♯m   D
You can call me Lucifer if you think you should.

            E5
I know I'm good, yeah.

Verse 2

| E | A | G | D/F♯ |

Ev'ry night I'm barrelhousin' till the moon is low.

| A | | G | D/F♯ | A/E | | E |

Shoutin' blues and payin' dues and throwin' way my dough.

A

Ramblin', gamblin', lovin', shovin',

| G | | D/F♯ |

Pro'ably won't end up with nothin'.

| A | | G | D/F♯ | A |

But at least I'll reap the seeds I ___ sow.

Chorus 2

| A/E | | E | F♯m | | D |

You can call me Lucifer if you think you should.

E5

I know I'm good, yeah. Yeah.

Guitar Solo

| E   A | G Gadd9 | C | **3/4** N.C. |

  Yeah.

| **4/4** E5 | | | | |

Verse 3

| E | A | | G | D/F♯ |

Funky water farmer's daughter gonna make a law.

| A | | G | D/F♯ | A/E | | E |

Lucy Blue Chi - cago Green I love 'em till they fall.

| | | A | G | | D/F♯ |

Courtin' all the lovely foxes,   brunette, redheads, goldilockses,

| A | | G | D/F♯ | A |

Takin' time to grind ___ my crosscut saw.

Chorus 3

Repeat Chorus 1

Outro

E5

(Yeah. Yeah. Yeah. Yeah.) ***Repeat and fade***
                                          w/ lead vocal ad lib.

Mainstreet

Words and Music by
Bob Seger

Melody:

I re-mem-ber stand-ing on __ the cor-ner at mid-night,

(Capo 1st fret)

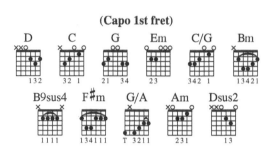

Intro

|D   C |G   Em |D   C/G |G   Em |

Verse 1

         D   C
I re - member standing on the corner at mid - night,

G Em   D   C
     Trying to get my courage up.

G Em   D   C
     There was this long, lovely dancer in a little club downtown,

G Em   D   C
     Loved to watch her do ___ her stuff.

Pre-Chorus 1

G Em   Bm   B9sus4
     Through the long, lonely nights,

Bm   B9sus4
She filled my sleep,

F#m   G   Em
     Her body softly swaying to that smok - y beat.

Chorus 1

G/A   D   C
Down on Main - street.

G Em   D   C
     Down on Main - street.

Verse 2

```
G  Em       D            C/G         G
   In the pool halls, the hustlers and the losers,

Em                       D          C/G
   Used to watch 'em through ___ the glass.

G  Em       D            C/G
   Well, I'd stand outside at clos - ing time

G  Em               D          C/G  G  Em
   Just to watch her walk on past.
```

Pre-Chorus 2

```
Bm                       B9sus4
   Unlike all the other la - dies,

          Bm              B9sus4
She looked so young and sweet,

   F#m               G             Em
As she made her way alone    down that emp - ty street.
```

Chorus 2

```
G/A             D      C
   Down on Main - street.

G  Em           D       C   G  Em
   Down on Main - street. ___     Oo.
```

Guitar Solo

```
‖:D  C/G │G   Em :‖ Play 4 times
```

Pre-Chorus 3

```
Bm                       B9sus4
   Sometimes even now,

          Bm              B9sus4
When I'm feeling lonely and beat,

F#m               G       Em
   I drift back in time ___ and I find my feet
```

Outro-Chorus

```
G/A             D      Am
   Down on Main - street.

 D  Am          D      Am
‖:     Down on Main - street.     :‖ Play 5 times

│D   Am │C    G  │Dsus2  D      ‖
```

Makin' Thunderbirds

Words and Music by
Bob Seger

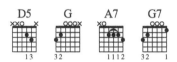

Intro

D5				
G		D5		
A7	G7	D5		

Verse 1

      D5
Well, the big line moved one mile an hour

So loud it really hurt.

   G   **D5**
The big line moved so loud it really hurt.

        A7   **G7**   **D5**
Back in '55 we were mak - in' Thunderbirds.

Verse 2

      D5
We filled conveyors, we met production.

Foremen didn't waste words.

   G   **D5**
We met production. Foreman didn't waste words.

         A7   **G7**   **D5**
We were young __ and proud, we were mak - in' Thunderbirds.

Chorus 1

                  D5
Well, we were mak - in' Thunderbirds,

We were makin' Thunderbirds.

              G
They were long __ and low and sleek and fast.

             D5
They were all __ you ever heard.

        A7   **G7**   **D5**
Back in '55 we were mak - in' Thunderbirds.

Piano Solo   *Repeat Verse 1 (Instrumental)*

Sax Solo   *Repeat Verse 1 (Instrumental)*

Verse 3

                  D5
Oh, now the years __ have flown and the plants have changed

And you're lucky if you work.

      G   **D5**
The big line moves but you're lucky if you work.

        A7   **G7**   **D5**
Back in '55 we were mak - in' Thunderbirds.

Chorus 2

                  D5
Well, we were mak - in' Thunderbirds,

We were makin' Thunderbirds.

              G
They were long __ and low and sleek and fast.

             D5
They were clas - sic in a word.

        A7   **G7**   **D5**
Back in '55 we were mak - in' Thunderbirds.

        A7   **G7**   **D5**
We were young __ and proud, we were mak - in' Thunderbirds.

        A7   **G7**   **D5**
We were young __ and sure, we were mak - in' Thunderbirds.

Outro   ‖: D5 | :‖ *Repeat and fade*

Night Moves

Words and Music by
Bob Seger

(Capo 1st fret)

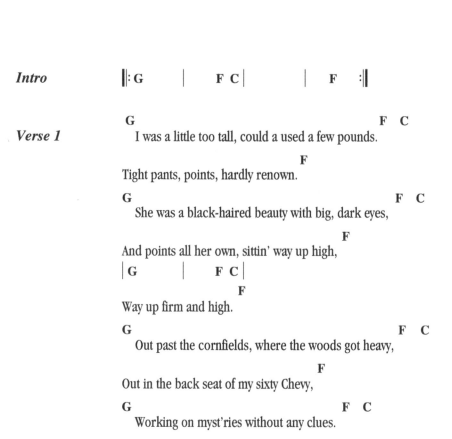

Intro ‖: G | F C | | F :‖

Verse 1

G   F   C
   I was a little too tall, could a used a few pounds.

                                    F
Tight pants, points, hardly renown.

G   F   C
   She was a black-haired beauty with big, dark eyes,

                                    F
And points all her own, sittin' way up high,

| G | | F C |

                 F
Way up firm and high.

G   F   C
   Out past the cornfields, where the woods got heavy,

                                    F
Out in the back seat of my sixty Chevy,

G   F   C
   Working on myst'ries without any clues.

Chorus 1

        D   **Em**   **D** **C**
Work-in' on our night moves,

        D   **Em**   **D** **C**
Try'n' to make some   front page, drive-in news.

        D   **Em**   **D** **C** **Cmaj7**
Work-in' on our night moves,

G   **F** **C**
In the summertime.

     F **G**   **F**   **C**   **F**
Mm,   in the sweet summertime.

Verse 2

G   **F** **C**
  We weren't in love. Oh, no, far from it.

                              F
We weren't searchin' for some pie-in-the-sky summit.

G   **F** **C**
We were just young and restless and bored,

            F
Living by the sword.

G   **F** **C**
And we'd steal away ev'ry chance we could,

                      F
To the backroom, to the alley, or the trusty woods.

G   **F** **C**
  I used her, she used me, but neither one cared,

We were gettin' our share.

Chorus 2

       D   **Em**   **D** **C**
Work-in' on our night moves,

       D   **Em**   **D** **C**
Tryin' to lose the   awkward teen-age blues.

       D   **Em**   **D** **C** **Cmaj7**
Work-in' on our night moves,   mm,

G   **F** **C**
And it was summertime.

      F **G**   **F**   **C**   **D**
Mm,   sweet summertime, sum-mertime.

Interlude 1 | **Em** | **D** | **G** |**G7** |

Bridge

    Cmaj7 **G**
And, oh, the wonder.

Cmaj7
We felt the lightning. Yeah,

F
And we waited on the thunder.

D   **G**
Waited on the thunder.

Verse 3

G
I awoke last night to the sound of thunder.

Cmaj7
"How far off?" I sat and wondered.

G
Started humming a song from nineteen-sixty-two.

Cmaj7   **Em**
Ain't it funny how the night moves?

C   **Em**
When you just don't seem to have as much to lose.

C   **Em**
Strange how the night moves

C **Cmaj7**
With autumn closing in.

Interlude 2

```
| G        |          |          |          | F  C|
|          |     F  | G        |          | F  C|
             Mm.          Night moves.
|          |     F  |          |
      Mm.
```

Outro

```
   G                        F   C
|: (Night moves.) Night moves.
                            F
(Night moves.) Yeah.        :|  Play 7 times
   G
(Night moves.) Night moves.
F   C                 D
      I remember. Oh!
```

Em
Ooh, ooh.

Bm
Ah, yeah, yeah, yeah, yeah.

Am   **C**   **G**
Ah,   ah.   I remember, I remember.

Nine Tonight

Words and Music by
Bob Seger

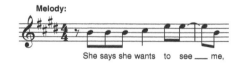

Melody:

She says she wants to see ___ me,

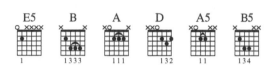

E5   B   A   D   A5   B5

Intro
| E5 | | B | | |
| A | | B | | |

Verse 1

E5   B
　She said she wants to see me,   she's tired of stayin' in.

A   E5
　She says she wants some rockin'. She's got the right ___ man.

　　　　　　　　　　　　　　B
I'm gonna take her ridin'   out past the edge of town,

A   E5
　Out where the wind's still racin' free on the heart - land.

Chorus 1

B   D   A   E5
　I'll be there nine tonight, nine tonight, nine tonight.

B   D   A   D   A
　Can't wait for nine tonight, nine tonight, nine to - night.

Verse 2	**E5** **B** I'm movin' into action, I'm shinin' up my wheels.
	A **E5** I'm tryin' hard to think of the right things to say, ___ now.
	B The sun is slowly sinkin', here comes a great big moon.
	A **E5** I'm startin' up my engine, it won't be long, ___ now.

Chorus 2	*Repeat Chorus 1*
Guitar Solo	*Repeat Verse 1 (Instrumental)*
Sax Solo	*Repeat Chorus 1 (Instrumental)*
Verse 3	*Repeat Verse 1*
Chorus 3	*Repeat Chorus 1*

Chorus 4	**E5** **A5** I'll be there nine tonight, ooh, nine tonight.
	B5 **A5** **E5** She might be my baby, she might be mine tonight.
	A5 Nine tonight, yeah, nine tonight.
	B5 **A5** **E5** She might be my baby, she might be mine tonight.
Outro-Chorus	**E5** **B** **A** ‖: Nine tonight, nine tonight, nine tonight,
	E5 She might be mine tonight :‖ ***Repeat and fade***

Ramblin' Gamblin' Man

Words and Music by
Bob Seger

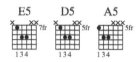

Intro | E5 | D5 |

       A5   **E5**
Yeah, ___ gonna tell my tale.

                      D5 A5   **E5**
Come on, come on, ___   give a listen,

Verse 1

                E5   **D5**
'Cause I was born lonely, down by the riverside,

           A5   **E5**
Learned to spin fortune wheels, throw dice.

                       D5
And I was just thirteen when I had to leave home,

          A5   **E5**
Knew I couldn't stick around, had to roam.

Verse 2

       E5   **D5**
I ain't good lookin', but you know I ain't shy,

         A5   **E5**
Ain't afraid to look you, girl, in the eye.

                     D5
So if you need some lovin', and you need it right away,

       A5   **E5**
Take a little time out and maybe I'll stay.

Chorus 1

        E5   **D5**
Then I got to ramble. (Ramblin' man.)

        A5   **E5**
Lord, I got to gamble. (Gamblin' man.)

                D5
Oh, I got to ramble. (Ramblin' man.)

        A5   **E5**
And I was born a ramblin', gamblin' man.

Guitar Solo 1 ‖: E5   D5 | | A5   E5 | :‖

Verse 3

        E5   **D5**
I hope you got money, I'm sure gonna need some.

        A5   **E5**
I ain't gon' run, I love you now, and I got to run.

                D5
I've got to keep movin', never gonna slow down.

        A5   **E5**
You can have your funky world, see you 'round.

Chorus 2

        E5   **D5**
I got to ramble. (Ramblin' man.)

        A5   **E5**
Yeah, I got to gamble. (Gamblin' man.)

                D5
Oh, I got to ramble. (Ramblin' man.)

        A5   **E5**
I was born a ramblin', gamblin' man.

Guitar Solo 2 ‖: E5   D5 | | A5   E5 | :‖ *Play 4 times*

Outro

      E5   **D5** **A5**   **E5**
‖: Ramblin' man,   gamblin' man. :‖ *Play 3 times*

E5   **D5**   **A5**   **E5**
All right.   Hey,   yeah.

The Real Love

Words and Music by
Bob Seger

Melody:

I think I've found a real love, _

(Capo 1st fret)

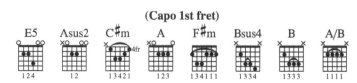

E5   Asus2   C#m   A   F#m   Bsus4   B   A/B

Intro
‖: E5 | | Asus2 | :‖

Verse 1
                          E5   **Asus2**
I think I've found a real love, genuine and true.

                E5
I think it's really come my way today, babe,

                   Asus2 E5 Asus2
I think it's really you.

Verse 2
                E5   **Asus2**
I remember moments looking in your eyes.

              E5
Could have sworn I saw the spark of love, babe,

         Asus2
Flickering in - side.

Chorus 1
         E5   **C#m**
I've been a - round and 'round this track,

        E5   **A**   **F#m** **Bsus4**
And the only thing I lack ___ is the real love.

Verse 3
B   **E5**   **Asus2**
 Ev'ry time I see you, ev'ry time we touch,

        E5
I can feel the way you feel for me, babe,

        Asus2
And it means so much.

GUITAR CHORD SONGBOOK

Chorus 2

         E5   C#m
And ev'ry time you look at me,

         E5   A
It's just the way it all should be

   F#m   Bsus4 B
In the real love.

Bridge

A   E5   B
  Oh, darlin', darlin', dar - lin',

A/B   E5
  Stay with me, stay.

A   E5   B
  I long to see you in the morn - ing sun ev'ry day, every day.

Guitar Solo

‖: E5 | |Asus2 | :‖

Verse 4

       E5   Asus2
So until that moment when I take your hand,

        E5
I'm gonna try to do my very best, babe,

            Asus2
To prove that I'm your man.

Chorus 3

        E5   C#m
I'm gonna do my very best,

E5   A   F#m   Bsus4
I'm not gonna rest ___ until we've got the real love.

B   E5
  Real love.

Outro-Chorus

  Asus2   E5
‖: Until we've got the real love. :‖ *Repeat and fade*

Rock and Roll Never Forgets

Words and Music by
Bob Seger

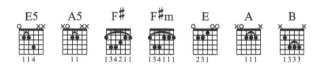

So you're a   lit - tle bit old - er

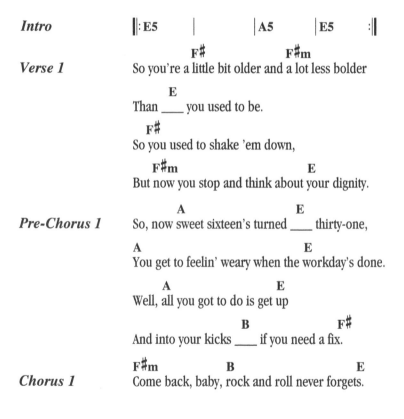

E5   A5   F#   F#m   E   A   B

Intro   ‖: E5 | |A5 |E5   :‖

Verse 1
        F#   **F#m**
So you're a little bit older and a lot less bolder

      E
Than ____ you used to be.

    F#
So you used to shake 'em down,

    F#m   **E**
But now you stop and think about your dignity.

Pre-Chorus 1
        A   **E**
So, now sweet sixteen's turned ____ thirty-one,

A   **E**
You get to feelin' weary when the workday's done.

    A   **E**
Well, all you got to do is get up

              B   **F#**
And into your kicks ____ if you need a fix.

Chorus 1
F#m   **B**   **E**
Come back, baby, rock and roll never forgets.

Verse 2

N.C.   F#
    You better get yourself a partner,

F#m   E
Go down to the concert or the local bar.

     F#
Check the local newspapers,

F#m   E
Chances are you won't have to go too far.

Pre-Chorus 2

         A   E
Yeah, the rafters will be ringin' 'cause the beat's so strong,

A   E
The crowd will be swaying and ___ singing along.

     A   E
And all you got to do is get in,

           B   F#
Into the mix ___ if you need a fix.

Chorus 2

         F#m   B   E
You can come back, baby, rock and roll never forgets.

Bridge

N.C.   A   E
    Oo, the band's still playing it ___ loud and lean.

A   E
Listen to the guitar play - er making its scream.

A   E   B
All you got to do is just ___ make that scene tonight.

Hey, tonight! Woo!

| *Guitar Solo* | |F# F#m| E | | F# | |
| | | F#m| E | | | |

Pre-Chorus 3
          A   E
Well, now ___ sweet sixteen's turned ___ thirty-one,

    A   E
Feel a little tired, feel - ing under the gun.

      A   E   B
Well, all of Chuck's children are out there, playing his licks.

             F#
Get into your kicks.

Chorus 3
      F#m   B   E
Then come back, baby, rock and roll never forgets.

        F#m   B   E
Said you can come back, baby, rock and roll never forgets.

       F#m   B   E N.C.
Oh, come back, baby, rock and roll never forgets. ___ Oo.

Interlude
E5   A5   E5
   Oh, yeah. Oh, yeah.

       A5   E5
Ha. Uh, huh. Uh, huh,

        E
Never forgets. ___ Oh, no.

     A   E
Oh, ___ no. Oo, never forgets.

          A E
Ah, yeah. Oo. ___ Oh, Lord.

Outro-
Guitar Solo
  ||: E | A | E | :|| *Repeat and fade*
                                                   w/ vocal ad lib.

Roll Me Away

Words and Music by
Bob Seger

Melody:

Took a   look _ down a   west - bound _ road. ____

C   Dm7/C   F/C   G   F   C/E   Dm   Am   Em

Intro   ‖: C | Dm7/C | C | F/C   :‖

Verse 1

    C   Dm7/C
Took a look down a westbound road.

            C   F/C
Right away, ____ I made my choice.

  C   Dm7/C
Headed out to my big two wheeler,

          C   F/C
I was tired ____ of my own voice.

  G   C
Took a bead on the northern plains

         F   C/E G
And just rolled ____ that power on.

Verse 2

```
      C                    F/C
      Twelve hours out of Mackinac city,

                    C                 F/C
      Stopped in a bar ____ to have a brew.

      C                  F/C
      Met a girl and we had a few drinks

                 C                      F/C
      And I told ____ her what I'd decided to do.

      G              F            C
      She looked out the window a long, ____ long moment,

                      F      C/E
      Then she looked in - to my eyes.

      G
      She didn't have to say a thing, I knew what she was thinkin'.
```

Chorus 1

```
      C    F/C
      Roll, ____ roll me away.

              C                F/C
      Won't you roll me away tonight.

      C            F/C
      I too am lost, I feel double crossed.

              C                       F/C
      And I'm sick of what's wrong and what's right.

      G            C
      We never even said a word.

                     F                 C/E
      We just walked out ____ and got on that bike.

      G                              C  F/C  C  F/C
      And we rolled, and we rolled clean out of sight.

      | C        | F/C      | C        | F/C      |
```

Bridge

```
      Dm                G        Dm            G
      We rolled across the high plains    deep into the mountains.

      Am            Em  F          G
      Felt so good to me,    fin'lly feelin' free.

      Dm                G        Dm            G
      Somewhere along a high road    the air began to turn cold.

      Am                      Em   F            G
      She said she missed her home.   I headed on a - lone, oh.
```

Interlude ‖: C |F/C |C |F/C   :‖ *Play 4 times*

Verse 3

C   Dm7/C
    Stood alone on a mountaintop

              C   F/C
Starin' out ___ at the Great Divide.

C   Dm7/C
    I could go east, I could go west.

              C   F/C
It was all ___ up to me to decide.

G   F   C
    Just then I saw a young hawk flyin'

        F   C/E
And my soul began to rise.

G
    And pretty soon my heart was singin'.

Chorus 2

C   F/C
    Roll, ___ roll me away,

              C   F/C
I'm gonna roll me away tonight.

C   F/C
    Gotta keep rollin', got - ta keep ridin',

              C   F/C
Keep search - in', till I find what's right.

G   C
    And as the sunset faded,

              F   C/E
I spoke to the faint - est first starlight.

G   C F/C C F/C
    And I said next time, next time we'll get it right.

Outro   ‖: C |F/C   :‖ *Repeat and fade w/ vocal ad lib.*

Rosalie

Words and Music by
Bob Seger

Melody:

She's quite the me - di - a - tor,

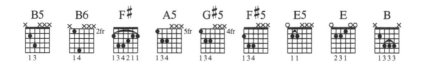

B5   B6   F#   A5   G#5   F#5   E5   E   B

Intro   ‖: B5   B6   B5   B6 | B5   :‖   *Play 6 times*

Verse 1
B5
She's quite the mediator,

B6   B5   B6 B5 B6 B5
 A smoother operator you will never see.

She'll see you later

B6   B5   B6 B5 B6 B5
 And no one dares disobey her open - ly.

Chorus 1
F#   A5   G#5 F#5 E5 A5 G#5 F#5 E5
 She knows music, I know music too, you see.

F#   A5   G#5 F#5 E5
 She's got the power, a girl teen queen Rosa - lie.

A5 G#5 F#5 E5   B5 B6 B5 B6   B5   B6 B5 B6 B5
 Rosalie, ___   Ros - alie.

Verse 2
B5
She's got the plastic,

B6   B5   B6   B5 B6 B5
 Comes from all the corners, corners of the world.

     B6   B5   B6 B5 B6 B5
So fantastic, she's ev'rybody's fav'rite little record girl.

Chorus 2

F♯   A5 G♯5 F♯5 E5 A5 G♯5 F♯5 E5
  She knows music, I know music too, you see.

F♯   A5 G♯5 F♯5 E5
  She's got the power, she's got the power, Rosa - lie,

A5 G♯5 F♯5 E5 B5 B6 B5 B6 B5 B6 B5 B6 B5
    Rosalie.   Ros - alie.

Interlude ‖: B5 B6 B5 F♯5 | B5 :‖

Bridge

E B E B E B F♯
Show me. Show me. Show me.

Guitar Solo ‖: B5 B6 B5 B6 | B5 :‖

B5 B6   B5 B6
  From Chattanoo - ga, to good old Bogalusa

    B5   B6 B5 B6 B5
You can hear 'em fine.

She makes her choices

B6   B5 B6 B5 B6 B5
  And then you best be smilin' when it's choosin' time.

Chorus 3

F♯   A5 G♯5 F♯5 E5 A5 G♯5 F♯5 E5
  She knows music, I know music too, you see.

F♯   A5 G♯5 F♯5 E5
  She's got the power, she's got the tower, Rosa - lie,

A5 G♯5 F♯5 E5 B5 B6 B5 B6 B5 B6 B5 B6 B5
    Rosalie.   Ros - alie.

F♯
  She knows music. She knows music. She knows music.

    B5 B6 B5 B6 B5 B6 B5 B6 B5
Rosalie. ____   Ros - alie.

Outro ‖: B5 B6 B5 B6 | B5 :‖   ‖

Satisfied

Words and Music by
Bob Seger

I need some wis - dom, _

(Capo 2nd fret)

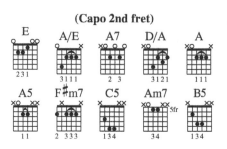

Verse 1

    E   A/E E
I need some wisdom,

               A/E E
I need some truth.

               A/E E
I need some beauty,

             A7
I need some proof.

             D/A A
And in the meantime,

             D/A E A/E E
I need a place to hide.

A/E B
    If I had you, babe,

A7   D/A E A/E E
  I'd be sat - isfied.

Verse 2

      E   A/E E
      Went to the ocean,

                    A/E E
Stood in the surf.

                A/E E
I felt the water,

             A7
I felt the earth.

             D/A A
I heard the angels,

             D/A E A/E E
They couldn't be denied.

A/E B
      If I had you, babe,

A5   D/A E A/E E
    I'd be sat - isfied.

Bridge

      A   F#m7
      Who's gonna believe me? I'm a broken down dog.

      E
      But, I can still snarl with the best.

      A   F#m7
      The train is leavin', we can catch it if we run.

         C5   Am7 B5
We can leave it all behind,   this utter emptiness.

| *Piano Solo* | |E   A/E E | A/E E | A/E E | | |

Piano Solo	|E A/E E	A/E E	A/E E		
	|A D/A A	D/A |E A/E E		
		B5	A	E		

Verse 3

```
E                    A/E  E
    You are the reason

                A/E  E
That I was born.

                A/E  E
You are the answer

              A7
I'm lookin' for.

              D/A  A
All of the others

              D/A   E   A/E  E
Just stood around and lied.

B5
    If I had you, babe,

A5                  E
    I'd be satisfied. ____ Oh.
```

Outro-Piano Solo

```
|E        A/E |E     A/E |E     A/E |E          |
|A5   D/A  A  |          |E     A/E |E          |
|B5          |A5         |E          |         ‖
```

Shakedown

from the Paramount Motion Picture
BEVERLY HILLS COP II

Words and Music by Keith Forsey,
Harold Faltermeyer and Bob Seger

Melody:

No mat-ter what ___ you think you've pulled ___

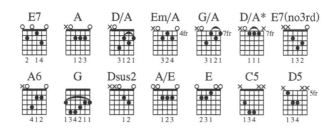

Intro   ‖: N.C.(E7) | | :‖   *Play 3 times*

         N.C.(E7)

Verse 1   No matter what you think you've pulled you'll find it's not enough.

        No matter who you think you know you won't get through.

        A   **D/A**   **Em/A**   **G/A D/A***
        It's a given L.A. law; someone's faster on the draw.

        N.C.(E7)
        No matter where you hide I'm comin' after you.

        E7(no 3rd)   **A6**   **E7(no3rd)**   **A6**

Verse 2   No matter how ___ the race is won it always ends ___ the same.

        E7(no3rd)   **A6**   **E7(no3rd) A6**
        Another room ___ without a view awaits down - town.

        A   **D/A Em/A**   **G/A D/A***
        You can shake me for a while; live it up in style.

        E7(no3rd)   **A6**   **E7(no3rd) A6**
        No matter what ___ you do I'm goin' to take you down.

Chorus 1

N.C.(E7)
Shakedown, breakdown, takedown;

Ev'rybody wants into the crowded light.

                                      G A
Breakdown, takedown, you're busted.

E7(no3rd)   Dsus2
Let down your guard, honey,

    E7(no3rd)   Dsus2
Just ___ about the time you think that it's all right.

E7(no3rd)   Dsus2   E7(no3rd)
Breakdown, take - down; you're bust - ed.

Interlude   ‖: A/E E | | A/E E | :‖

Verse 3

               E7(no3rd)   A6   E7(no3rd) A6
This is the town ___ where ev'ry - one is reachin' for ___ the top.

            E7(no3rd)   A6   E7(no3rd) A6
This is a place ___ where second best will never do.

      A   D/A   Em/A   G/A D/A
It's O. - K. to want to shine, but once you step across that line,

          E7(no3rd)   A6   E7(no3rd) A6
No matter where you hide I'm comin' after you.

Chorus 2

N.C.(E7)
Shakedown, breakdown, takedown;

Ev'rybody wants into the crowded light.

                                        G A
Breakdown, takedown, you're busted.

E7(no3rd)   Dsus2
Shakedown, break - down, honey,

    E7(no3rd)   Dsus2
Just ___ about the time you think that it's all right.

E7(no3rd)   Dsus2   E7(no 3rd)
Breakdown, take - down; you're bust - ed.

Guitar Solo

```
|C5         |D5         |C5         |          |          |
|D5         |           |N.C.(E7)   |          |          |
|           |           |           |          |          |
|           |G    A     |E7(no3rd)  |Dsus2     |          |
|E7(no3rd)  |Dsus2      |E7(no3rd)  |Dsus2     |          |
|E7(no3rd)  |           |           |          |          |
```

Chorus 3

N.C.
Shakedown, breakdown, takedown;

Ev'rybody wants into the crowded light.

                                        G A
Breakdown, takedown, you're busted.

E7(no3rd)   **Dsus2**
Shakedown, break - down, honey,

    E7(no3rd)   **Dsus2**
Just ___ about the time you think that it's all right.

E7(no3rd)   **Dsus2**   **E7(no3rd) G A**
Breakdown, take - down; you're bust - ed.

Chorus 4

N.C.(E7)
Shakedown, breakdown, takedown;

Ev'rybody wants into the crowded light.

                                        G A
Breakdown, takedown, you're busted.

E7(no3rd)   **Dsus2**
Let down your guard, honey,

    E7(no3rd)   **Dsus2**
Just ___ about the time you think that it's all right.

E7(no3rd)   **Dsus2**   **E7(no3rd) G A**
Breakdown, take - down; you're bust - ed.

Outro

Repeat Chorus 1 till fade

Still the Same

Words and Music by
Bob Seger

Melody:

You al - ways won __

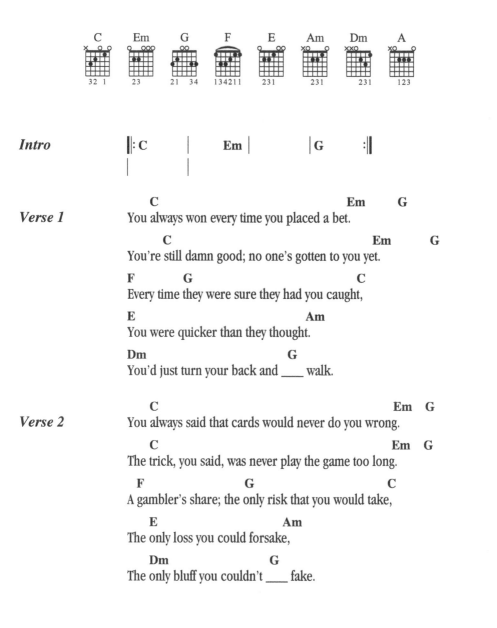

C   Em   G   F   E   Am   Dm   A

Intro

‖: C | Em | | G :‖
| |

Verse 1

    C   Em   G
You always won every time you placed a bet.

      C   Em   G
You're still damn good; no one's gotten to you yet.

F   G   C
Every time they were sure they had you caught,

E   Am
You were quicker than they thought.

Dm   G
You'd just turn your back and ___ walk.

Verse 2

    C   Em G
You always said that cards would never do you wrong.

    C   Em G
The trick, you said, was never play the game too long.

  F   G   C
A gambler's share; the only risk that you would take,

  E   Am
The only loss you could forsake,

  Dm   G
The only bluff you couldn't ___ fake.

Chorus 1
                                            C
And you're still the same.

    E   A
I caught up with you yesterday.

                 Dm
Moving game to game;

                       G
No one standing in your way.

                C
Turning on the charm

E   A
Long enough to get you by.

                     Dm   G
You're still the same, ____ you still aim ____ high.

Piano Solo   ‖: C | | Em | G   :‖

Verse 3
F   G   C
There you stood; ev'rybody watched you play.

E   Am
I just turned and walked away.

Dm   G
I had nothing left to say.

Chorus 2

                                    C
'Cause you're still the same.

                                               Em   G
(Still the same, baby, babe, you're still the same.)

                       C
You're still the same.

                                               Em   G
(Still the same, baby, babe, you're still the same.)

                         C
Moving game to game.

                                             Em   G
(Still the same, baby, babe, you're still the same.)

                            C
Some things never change.

                                           Em   G
(Still the same, baby, babe, you're still the same.)

                         C
Ah, you're still the same.

                                           Em   G
(Still the same, baby, babe, you're still the same.)

                    C
Still the same.

                                           Em   G
(Still the same, baby, babe, you're still the same.)   *Fade out*

Sunspot Baby

Words and Music by
Bob Seger

Melody:

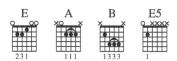

She packed up her bags _

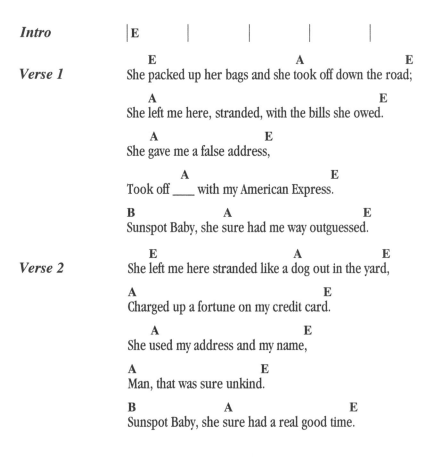

E   A   B   E5

231   1 1 1   1 3 3 3   1

Intro | E | | | | | |

Verse 1

E   A   E
She packed up her bags and she took off down the road;

A   E
She left me here, stranded, with the bills she owed.

A   E
She gave me a false address,

A   E
Took off ____ with my American Express.

B   A   E
Sunspot Baby, she sure had me way outguessed.

Verse 2

E   A   E
She left me here stranded like a dog out in the yard,

A   E
Charged up a fortune on my credit card.

A   E
She used my address and my name,

A   E
Man, that was sure unkind.

B   A   E
Sunspot Baby, she sure had a real good time.

Chorus 1

   A   E
I looked in Miami, I looked in Negril.

    A   E
The closest I came was a month ___ old bill.

   A   E
I checked the Bahamas and they said she was gone.

  B
Can't understand why she did me so wrong.

Verse 3

          E   A   E
But she packed up her bags, she took off down the road;

   A   E
She said she was going to visit sister Flo.

   A   E
She used my address and my name,

   A   E
And man, that was sure unkind.

  B   A   E
Sunspot Baby, I'm gonna catch up some time.

Sure had a real good time.

Guitar Solo

	E	A	E		
	A		E		
	A	E	A	E	
	B	A	E		

Chorus 2   *Repeat Chorus 1*

                          E   A   E
Verse 4   But she packed up her bags and she took off down the road;

                      A   E
                  She left me here, stranded, with the bills she owed.

                      A   E
                  She used my address and my name,

                  A   E
                  Put my credit to shame.

                  B   A   E
                  Sunspot Baby, sure had a real good time.

                      B   A   E
                  Oh, Sunspot Baby, she sure had a real good time.

                        B   A   E5
                  Yeah, Sunspot Baby, I'm gonna catch up sometime, ___ sometime. Oh!

Outro-
Guitar Solo | E | A | E | |
                                                  Yeah!   *Oo!*

                  | A | | E | |
                                        Goin' track you down.   *Huh!*

                  | A | E | A | E |
                  ||: B | A | E | :||
                  | B | A | E5 | |
                  | ||

Travelin' Man

Words and Music by
Bob Seger

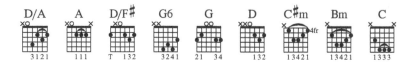

D/A	A	D/F♯	G6	G	D	C♯m	Bm	C
3121	111	T 132	3241	21 34	132	13421	13421	1333

Verse 1

  D/A   A D/A   A
Up with the sun, ___ gone with the wind.

  D/A   A   D/F♯ G6
She always said ___ I was la - zy.

  D/A   A D/A   A
Leavin' my home, ___ leavin' my friends.

  D/A   A   G D/F♯
Runnin' when things ___ get too cra - zy.

Pre-Chorus 1

  D   C♯m
Out to the road, out 'neath the stars.

  Bm   A   D/A A
Feelin' the breeze, passin' the cars.

Verse 2

  D/A   A D/A   A
Women have come, ___ women have gone.

  D/A   A   D/F♯   G6
Ev'ryone try - in' to cage ___ me.

  D/A   A D/A   A
Some were so sweet ___ I barely got free.

  D/A   A   G   D/F♯
Others they on - ly enraged ___ me.

Pre-Chorus 2

    D   C#m
Sometimes at night I see their faces.

    C   Bm
I feel the traces they've left on my soul.

Chorus 1

    D/A   A
Those are the mem'ries that make me a wealthy soul.

    D/A   A
Those are the mem'ries that make me a wealthy soul.

Verse 3

    D/A   A   D/A   A
Travelin' man, ___ love when I can.

    D/A   A   D/F#   G6
Turn loose my hand ___ 'cause I'm go - in' tonight.

    D/A   A   D/A   A
Travelin' man, ___ catch if you can.

     D/A   A   G   D/F#
But sooner than lat - er I'm go - in',   travelin' man.

Guitar Solo

| D/A   A | D/A   A | D/A   A | D |
     Yeah.   Awe.   Hey,

| G | D/A   A | D/A   A | D/A   A |
 A travelin' man   yes, I am.

| G | D/F# |

Pre-Chorus 3

    D   C#m
Sometimes at night I see their faces.

    Bm   A   D/A
I feel the traces they've left on my soul.

Outro-Chorus

    D/A   A
Those are the mem'ries that make me a wealthy soul.

    D   N.C.   A
  Those are the mem'ries that make me a wealthy   soul.

Turn the Page

Words and Music by
Bob Seger

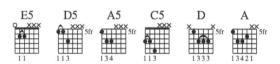

E5	D5	A5	C5	D	A
1 1	1 1 3	1 3 4	1 1 3	1 3 3 3	1 3 4 2 1

Intro |E5 | | | |

Verse 1
　　　　　　　　　　E5
On a long ___ and lonesome highway, east of Omaha,

　　　　　　　　　　D5
You can listen to the engine moanin' out his one note song.

　　　　　　　　　　A5　　　　　　　　　　　　　　　　　　　　**E5**
You can think about the woman or the girl you knew the night before.

Verse 2
　　　　　　　　　　E5
But, your thoughts will soon be wandering the way they always do,

　　　　　　　　　　D5
When you are ridin' sixteen hours and there's nothin' much to do,

　　　　　　　　　　A5
And you don't ___ feel much like ridin',

　　　　　　　　　　　　　　　　E5
You just wish the trip was through.　　Mm.

Chorus 1

               D5   **E5**
Say, here I am ___ on the road again.

               D5   **E5**
There I am ___ up on the stage.

               D5   **A5**
Here I go ___ playin' star ___ again.

               C5 D5   **E5**
There I go, ___   turn the page, ___ ah.

Verse 3

               E5
Well, you walk ___ into a restaurant strung out from the road,

               D5
And you feel ___ the eyes upon you as you're shakin' off the cold.

               A5   **E5**
You pretend ___ it doesn't bother you, but you just want to explode.

Verse 4

               E5
Most times you can't hear 'em talk, other times you can.

               D5
All the same old clichés, "Is that a woman or a man?"

               A5   **E5**
And you al - ways seem out numbered, you don't dare make a stand.

Chorus 2

               D5   **E5**
Ah, here I am, ___ on the road again.

               D5   **E5**
There I am, ___ up on the stage.

               D5   **A5**
Ah, here I go, ___ playin' star ___ again.

               C5 D5   **E5**
There I go, ___   turn the page, ___ ah.

	E5
Verse 5	Out there in the spotlight you're a million miles away.

D5

Ev'ry ounce of energy you try to give away,

     A5   **E5**

As the sweat pours out your body like the music that you play.

	E5
Verse 6	Later in the ev'ning, as you lie awake in bed,

        D

With the echoes from the amplifiers ringin' in your head,

     A   **E5**

You smoke the day's last cigarette, rememb'rin' what she said.

Chorus 3   *Repeat Chorus 2*

	D5 **E5**
Chorus 4	Now, here I am, ___ on the road again.

D5   **E5**

There I am, ___ up on ___ the stage.

D5   **A5**

Here I go, ___ playin' star ___ again.

C5 **D5**   **E5**

There I go, ___   there I go.

Wreck This Heart

Words and Music by
Bob Seger

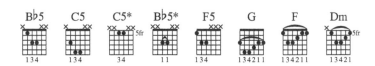

I feel a cold wind blow-in' all ___

Bb5   C5   C5*   Bb5*   F5   G   F   Dm

Intro   ‖: Bb5 C5 C5* Bb5* C5* F5 | :‖ *Play 4 times*

Verse 1
       Bb5 C5   C5* Bb5* C5* F5
I feel a cold ___ wind blow - in'   all ____ over me,

          Bb5 C5   C5* Bb5* C5* F5
I feel the dark ___ clouds start - in'   to   form.

     Bb5 C5   C5* Bb5* C5* F5
The trees ___ are bare, ___   the grass is brown,

        G   F
Another early winter Michigan storm.

Bb5 C5   C5* Bb5* C5* F5
Ev - 'rything I do   is   just a little wrong.

Bb5 C5   C5* Bb5* C5* F5
Ev - 'ry day for me is   the same.

    Bb5 C5   C5* Bb5* C5* F5
Ev'ry - one I know ___ is   get - tin' in my face

    G   F
And I only got myself to blame.

Chorus 1
              C5   Bb5 F
I think I'm gonna wreck this   heart,

C5   Bb5 F
Wreck this   heart,

C5   Bb5 F   Bb5 C5 C5* Bb5* C5* F5
Wreck this   heart after a while.

| Bb5 C5 C5* Bb5* C5* F5 | |

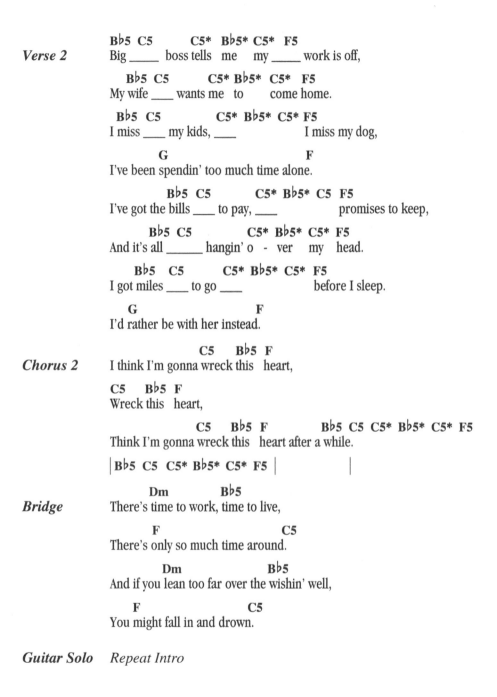

Verse 2

B♭5 C5   C5* B♭5* C5* F5
Big _____ boss tells me my _____ work is off,

  B♭5 C5   C5* B♭5* C5* F5
My wife ____ wants me to   come home.

  B♭5 C5   C5* B♭5* C5* F5
I miss ____ my kids, ____   I miss my dog,

      G   F
I've been spendin' too much time alone.

         B♭5 C5   C5* B♭5* C5 F5
I've got the bills ____ to pay, ____   promises to keep,

     B♭5 C5   C5* B♭5* C5* F5
And it's all _____ hangin' o - ver my head.

    B♭5   C5   C5* B♭5* C5* F5
I got miles ____ to go ____   before I sleep.

     G   F
I'd rather be with her instead.

Chorus 2

                C5   B♭5 F
I think I'm gonna wreck this heart,

C5   B♭5 F
Wreck this heart,

              C5   B♭5 F   B♭5 C5 C5* B♭5* C5* F5
Think I'm gonna wreck this heart after a while.

| B♭5 C5 C5* B♭5* C5* F5 | | |

Bridge

    Dm   B♭5
There's time to work, time to live,

     F   C5
There's only so much time around.

      Dm   B♭5
And if you lean too far over the wishin' well,

    F   C5
You might fall in and drown.

Guitar Solo   *Repeat Intro*

Verse 3

    C5   F5
Am I talkin' too fast, am I hard to hear?

       C5   F5
Have you understood a word that I've said?

     C5   F5
Let me put it to you this way

   G   F
And underlined in red.

C5   F5
Order me a case of your Southern soul,

   C5   F5
And let me out tonight.

    C5   F5
I need a good, long ride on your rodeo,

   G   F
And ev'rything 'll be alright.

Chorus 3

               C5   Bb5 F
And then I'm gonna wreck this   heart,

C5   Bb5 F
Wreck this   heart,

C5   Bb5 F   Bb5 C5 C5* Bb5* C5* F5
Wreck this   heart after a while.

      C5   Bb5 F
I'm gonna wreck this   heart.

      C5   Bb5 F
I'm gonna wreck this   heart.

          C5   Bb5 F   Bb5 C5 C5* Bb5* C5* F5
Think I'm gonna wreck this   heart after a while.

Outro-
Guitar Solo   *Repeat Intro*

Wait for Me

Words and Music by
Bob Seger

Melody:

I will an - swer the wind.

(Capo 1st fret)

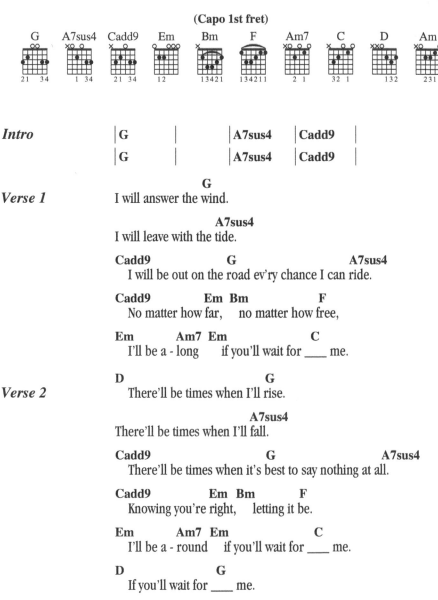

Intro

| | | |G| | | |A7sus4 |Cadd9 | |
| |G| | | |A7sus4 |Cadd9 | |

Verse 1

         G
I will answer the wind.

         A7sus4
I will leave with the tide.

Cadd9   G   A7sus4
 I will be out on the road ev'ry chance I can ride.

Cadd9   Em Bm   F
 No matter how far, no matter how free,

Em   Am7 Em   C
 I'll be a - long if you'll wait for ___ me.

Verse 2

D   G
 There'll be times when I'll rise.

         A7sus4
There'll be times when I'll fall.

Cadd9   G   A7sus4
 There'll be times when it's best to say nothing at all.

Cadd9   Em Bm   F
 Knowing you're right, letting it be.

Em   Am7 Em   C
 I'll be a - round if you'll wait for ___ me.

D   G
 If you'll wait for ___ me.

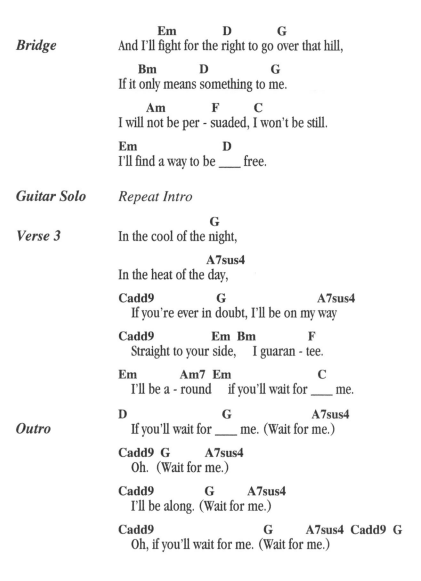

Bridge

      Em   D   G
And I'll fight for the right to go over that hill,

     Bm   D   G
If it only means something to me.

       Am   F   C
I will not be per - suaded, I won't be still.

Em   D
I'll find a way to be ___ free.

Guitar Solo   *Repeat Intro*

Verse 3

                G
In the cool of the night,

             A7sus4
In the heat of the day,

Cadd9   G   A7sus4
  If you're ever in doubt, I'll be on my way

Cadd9   Em Bm   F
  Straight to your side,   I guaran - tee.

Em   Am7 Em   C
  I'll be a - round   if you'll wait for ___ me.

Outro

D   G   A7sus4
  If you'll wait for ___ me. (Wait for me.)

Cadd9 G   A7sus4
  Oh. (Wait for me.)

Cadd9   G   A7sus4
  I'll be along. (Wait for me.)

Cadd9   G   A7sus4 Cadd9 G
  Oh, if you'll wait for me. (Wait for me.)

We've Got Tonight

Words and Music by
Bob Seger

Melody:

I know it's late. ___

(Capo 4th fret)

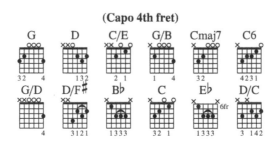

G D C/E G/B Cmaj7 C6
G/D D/F# B♭ C E♭ D/C

Intro
‖: G |D |C/E |D   :‖

Verse 1
                  G D   **C/E**
I know it's late. ____   I know you're wea - ry.

D   **G/B Cmaj7 C6**   **G**
  I know your plans ___   don't include me.

D   **G Cmaj7 C6**   **G**
  Still, here we are, ___   both of us lone - ly,

                  Cmaj7 C6   **G**
Longing for shelter   from all that we see.

D   **G/B Cmaj7 C6**   **G/D**
  Why should we wor - ry?   No one will care, ___ girl.

D   **G/B**   **Cmaj7 C6**   **G/D**
  Look at the stars ___ babe,   so far away.

Chorus 1
D   **G Cmaj7 C6**   **G**
  We've got tonight. ___   Who needs tomor - row?

             G/B   **Cmaj7 C6**   **G**
We've got tonight, ___ babe.   Why don't you ___ stay?

                              G   D/F#   **C/E**
Verse 2   Deep in my soul ___   I've been so lone - ly.

              D   **G   Cmaj7   C6   G**
              All of my hopes ___   fading away.

              D   **G   Cmaj7   C6   G**
              I've longed for love ___   like ev'ryone else ___ does.

                                      Cmaj7   C6   G
              I know I'll keep searching   even after today.

              D   **G/B   Cmaj7   C6   G/D**
              So there it is, ___ girl.   I've said it all ___ now.

              D   **G/B   Cmaj7   C6   G/D**
              And here we are, ___ babe.   What do you say?

Chorus 2   *Repeat Chorus 1*

              B♭   **G**
Bridge   I know it's late, I know you're weary.

              B♭   **G**
              Ooh, I know your plans don't include me.

                          C   E♭   **G**
              Still, here we are,   both of us lonely,

              Cmaj7 C6   G   Cmaj7 C6 G
              Both of us lonely.

                              G   Cmaj7   C6   **G**
Chorus 3   ‖: We've got tonight. ___   Who needs tomor - row?

                          Cmaj7   C6   G
              Let's make it last,   let's find a way.

              D   **G   Cmaj7   C6   G**
              Turn out the light, ___   come take my hand, now.

                            G/B   Cmaj7   C6   G
              We've got tonight, ___ babe.   Why don't you stay? :‖ *Play 3 times*

              Cmaj7 C6 G/D D   **D/C   G**
Outro   Oh. _____ Oh,   why don't ___ you ___ stay?

You'll Accomp'ny Me

Words and Music by
Bob Seger

Melody:

A gyp-sy wind is blow-ing   warm _to - night. _

A   E5   A/E   D   E

Intro   ‖: A   E5 |A/E   E5   :‖ *Play 4 times*

Verse 1

    A   E5   A/E   E5
A gyp - sy wind is blowing warm to - night.

    A   E5   A/E   E5
The sky is starlit and the time is right.

    A   E5   A/E   E5
And still you're tellin' me you have ____ to go.

    A   E5   A/E   E5
Before you leave, there's something you should know.

A E5   A/E E5   A   E5 A/E E5
  Yeah,   something you should know, ____ babe.

Verse 2

    A   E5   A/E   E5
I've seen you smiling in the sum - mer sun.

    A   E5   A/E   E5
I've seen your long hair flying when you run.

    A   E5   A/E   E5
I've made my mind up that it's meant to be.

    A   E5   A/E   E5
Some - day, lady, you'll ac - comp'ny me.

GUITAR CHORD SONGBOOK

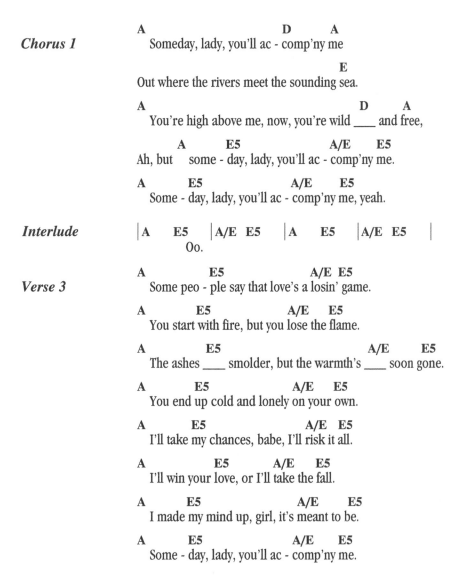

Chorus 1

A   D   A
Someday, lady, you'll ac - comp'ny me

                                      E
Out where the rivers meet the sounding sea.

A   D   A
You're high above me, now, you're wild ___ and free,

      A   E5   A/E   E5
Ah, but   some - day, lady, you'll ac - comp'ny me.

A   E5   A/E   E5
Some - day, lady, you'll ac - comp'ny me, yeah.

Interlude

|A   E5 |A/E E5 |A   E5 |A/E E5 |
       Oo.

Verse 3

A   E5   A/E E5
Some peo - ple say that love's a losin' game.

A   E5   A/E   E5
You start with fire, but you lose the flame.

A   E5   A/E   E5
The ashes ___ smolder, but the warmth's ___ soon gone.

A   E5   A/E   E5
You end up cold and lonely on your own.

A   E5   A/E   E5
I'll take my chances, babe, I'll risk it all.

A   E5   A/E   E5
I'll win your love, or I'll take the fall.

A   E5   A/E   E5
I made my mind up, girl, it's meant to be.

A   E5   A/E   E5
Some - day, lady, you'll ac - comp'ny me.

Chorus 2

A   D   A
Someday, lady, you'll ac - comp'ny me.

                                           E
It's written down somewhere, it's got to be.

A   D   A
You're high above me flyin' wild and free,

            E5   A/E   E5
Oh, but some - day, lady, you'll ac - comp'ny me.

A   E5   A/E   E5
Some - day, lady, you'll ac - comp'ny me.

Chorus 3

A   D   A
Someday, lady, you'll ac - comp'ny me

                                         E
Out where the rivers meet the sounding sea.

A   D   A
I feel it in my soul, it's meant to be.

            E5   A/E   E5
Oh, some - day, lady, you'll ac - comp'ny me.

A   E5   A/E   E5
Some - day, lady, you'll ac - comp'ny me.

You will accomp'ny me.

Outro

   A E5 A/E E5
‖: (Oo, hoo,)

   A E5   A/E   E5
(Oo, hoo, you'll ac - comp'ny me.) :‖ *Repeat and fade*
                                            w/ lead vocal ad lib.

This series will help you play your favorite songs quickly and easily. Just follow the tab and listen to the CD to hear how the guitar should sound, and then play along using the separate backing tracks. Mac or PC users can also slow down the tempo without changing pitch by using the CD in their computer. The melody and lyrics are included in the book so that you can sing or simply follow along.

INCLUDES TAB

. ROCK
0699570...................................$16.99

. ACOUSTIC
0699569...................................$16.95

. HARD ROCK
0699573...................................$16.95

. POP/ROCK
0699571...................................$16.99

. MODERN ROCK
0699574...................................$16.99

. '90s ROCK
0699572•.................................$16.99

. BLUES
0699575...................................$16.95

. ROCK
0699585...................................$14.99

. PUNK ROCK
0699576...................................$14.95

0. ACOUSTIC
0699586...................................$16.95

1. EARLY ROCK
599579....................................$14.95

2. POP/ROCK
0699587...................................$14.95

13. FOLK ROCK
00699581.................................$15.99

14. BLUES ROCK
00699582.................................$16.95

15. R&B
00699583.................................$14.95

16. JAZZ
00699584.................................$15.95

17. COUNTRY
00699588.................................$15.95

18. ACOUSTIC ROCK
00699577.................................$15.95

19. SOUL
00699578.................................$14.99

20. ROCKABILLY
00699580.................................$14.95

21. YULETIDE
00699602.................................$14.95

22. CHRISTMAS
00699600.................................$15.95

23. SURF
00699635.................................$14.95

24. ERIC CLAPTON
00699649.................................$17.99

25. LENNON & McCARTNEY
00699642.................................$16.99

26. ELVIS PRESLEY
00699643.................................$14.95

27. DAVID LEE ROTH
00699645.................................$16.95

28. GREG KOCH
00699646.................................$14.95

29. BOB SEGER
00699647.................................$15.99

30. KISS
00699644.................................$16.99

31. CHRISTMAS HITS
00699652.................................$14.95

32. THE OFFSPRING
00699653.................................$14.95

33. ACOUSTIC CLASSICS
00699656.................................$16.95

34. CLASSIC ROCK
00699658.................................$16.95

35. HAIR METAL
00699660.................................$16.95

36. SOUTHERN ROCK
00699661.................................$16.95

37. ACOUSTIC METAL
00699662......................$16.95

38. BLUES
00699663......................$16.95

39. '80s METAL
00699664......................$16.99

40. INCUBUS
00699668......................$17.95

41. ERIC CLAPTON
00699669......................$16.95

42. 2000s ROCK
00699670......................$16.99

43. LYNYRD SKYNYRD
00699681......................$17.95

44. JAZZ
00699689......................$14.99

45. TV THEMES
00699718......................$14.95

46. MAINSTREAM ROCK
00699722......................$16.95

47. HENDRIX SMASH HITS
00699723......................$19.95

48. AEROSMITH CLASSICS
00699724......................$17.99

49. STEVIE RAY VAUGHAN
00699725......................$17.99

51. ALTERNATIVE '90s
00699727......................$14.99

52. FUNK
00699728......................$14.95

53. DISCO
00699729......................$14.99

54. HEAVY METAL
00699730......................$14.95

55. POP METAL
00699731......................$14.95

56. FOO FIGHTERS
00699749......................$14.95

57. SYSTEM OF A DOWN
00699751......................$14.95

58. BLINK-182
00699772......................$14.95

60. 3 DOORS DOWN
00699774......................$14.95

61. SLIPKNOT
00699775......................$16.99

62. CHRISTMAS CAROLS
00699798......................$12.95

63. CREEDENCE CLEARWATER REVIVAL
00699802......................$16.99

64. OZZY OSBOURNE
00699803......................$16.99

65. THE DOORS
00699806......................$16.99

66. THE ROLLING STONES
00699807......................$16.95

67. BLACK SABBATH
00699808......................$16.99

68. PINK FLOYD – DARK SIDE OF THE MOON
00699809......................$16.99

69. ACOUSTIC FAVORITES
00699810......................$14.95

70. OZZY OSBOURNE
00699805......................$16.99

71. CHRISTIAN ROCK
00699824......................$14.95

72. ACOUSTIC '90s
00699827......................$14.95

73. BLUESY ROCK
00699829......................$16.99

74. PAUL BALOCHE
00699831......................$14.95

75. TOM PETTY
00699882......................$16.99

76. COUNTRY HITS
00699884......................$14.95

77. BLUEGRASS
00699910......................$14.99

78. NIRVANA
00700132......................$16.99

79. NEIL YOUNG
00700133......................$24.99

80. ACOUSTIC ANTHOLOGY
00700175......................$19.95

81. ROCK ANTHOLOGY
00700176......................$22.99

82. EASY ROCK SONGS
00700177......................$12.99

83. THREE CHORD SONGS
00700178......................$16.99

84. STEELY DAN
00700200......................$16.99

85. THE POLICE
00700269......................$16.99

86. BOSTON
00700465......................$16.99

87. ACOUSTIC WOMEN
00700763......................$14.99

88. GRUNGE
00700467......................$19.99

90. CLASSICAL POP
00700469......................$14.99

91. BLUES INSTRUMENTALS
00700505......................$14.99

92. EARLY ROCK INSTRUMENTALS
00700506......................$14.99

93. ROCK INSTRUMENTALS
00700507......................$16.99

95. BLUES CLASSICS
00700509......................$14.99

96. THIRD DAY
00700560......................$14.95

97. ROCK BAND
00700703......................$14.99

98. ROCK BAND
00700704......................$14.95

99. ZZ TOP
00700762......................$16.99

100. B.B. KING
00700466......................$14.99

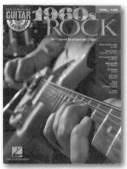

*Prices, contents, and availability
subject to change without notice.*

HAL•LEONARD®
CORPORATION
7777 W. BLUEMOUND RD. P.O. BOX 13819
MILWAUKEE, WISCONSIN 53213

**For audio samples and
complete songlists,
visit Hal Leonard online at
www.halleonard.com**

Guitar Chord Songbooks

Each book includes complete lyrics, chord symbols, and guitar chord diagrams.

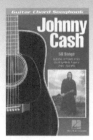
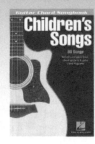

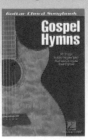

Acoustic Hits
More than 60 songs: Against the Wind • Name • One • Southern Cross • Take Me Home, Country Roads • Teardrops on My Guitar • Who'll Stop the Rain • Ziggy Stardust • and more.
00701787 ....$14.99

Acoustic Rock
80 acoustic favorites: Blackbird • Blowin' in the Wind • Layla • Maggie May • Me and Julio down by the Schoolyard • Pink Houses • and more.
00699540................................$21.99

Alabama
50 of Alabama's best: Angels Among Us • The Closer You Get • If You're Gonna Play in Texas (You Gotta Have a Fiddle in the Band) • Mountain Music • When We Make Love • and more.
00699914................................$14.95

The Beach Boys
59 favorites: California Girls • Don't Worry Baby • Fun, Fun, Fun • Good Vibrations • Help Me Rhonda • Wouldn't It Be Nice • dozens more!
00699566................................$19.99

The Beatles
100 more Beatles hits: Lady Madonna • Let It Be • Ob-La-Di, Ob-La-Da • Paperback Writer • Revolution • Twist and Shout • When I'm Sixty-Four • and more.
00699562................................$17.99

Bluegrass
Over 40 classics: Blue Moon of Kentucky • Foggy Mountain Top • High on a Mountain Top • Keep on the Sunny Side • Wabash Cannonball • The Wreck of the Old '97 • and more.
00702585................................$14.99

Johnny Cash
58 Cash classics: A Boy Named Sue • Cry, Cry, Cry • Daddy Sang Bass • Folsom Prison Blues • I Walk the Line • Ring of Fire • Solitary Man • and more.
00699648................................$17.99

Children's Songs
70 songs for kids: Alphabet Song • Bingo • The Candy Man • Eensy Weensy Spider • Puff the Magic Dragon • Twinkle, Twinkle Little Star • and more.
00699539................................$16.99

Christmas Carols
80 Christmas carols: Angels We Have Heard on High • The Holly and the Ivy • I Saw Three Ships • Joy to the World • O Holy Night • and more.
00699536................................$12.99

Christmas Songs
80 songs: All I Want for Christmas Is My Two Front Teeth • Baby, It's Cold Outside • Jingle Bell Rock • Mistletoe and Holly • Sleigh Ride • and more.
00119911................................$14.99

Eric Clapton
75 of Slowhand's finest: I Shot the Sheriff • Knockin' on Heaven's Door • Layla • Strange Brew • Tears in Heaven • Wonderful Tonight • and more.
00699567 ....$19.99

Classic Rock
80 rock essentials: Beast of Burden • Cat Scratch Fever • Hot Blooded • Money • Rhiannon • Sweet Emotion • Walk on the Wild Side • and more.
00699598 ....$18.99

Coffeehouse Hits
57 singer-songwriter hits: Don't Know Why • Hallelujah • Meet Virginia • Steal My Kisses • Torn • Wonderwall • You Learn • and more.
00703318 ....$14.99

Country
80 country standards: Boot Scootin' Boogie • Crazy • Hey, Good Lookin' • Sixteen Tons • Through the Years • Your Cheatin' Heart • and more.
00699534 ....$17.99

Country Favorites
Over 60 songs: Achy Breaky Heart (Don't Tell My Heart) • Brand New Man • Gone Country • The Long Black Veil • Make the World Go Away • and more.
00700609 ....$14.99

Country Hits
40 classics: As Good As I Once Was • Before He Cheats • Cruise • Follow Your Arrow • God Gave Me You • The House That Built Me • Just a Kiss • Making Memories of Us • Need You Now • Your Man • and more.
00140859 ....$14.99

Country Standards
60 songs: By the Time I Get to Phoenix • El Paso • The Gambler • I Fall to Pieces • Jolene • King of the Road • Put Your Hand in the Hand • A Rainy Night in Georgia • and more.
00700608 ....$12.95

Cowboy Songs
Over 60 tunes: Back in the Saddle Again • Happy Trails • Home on the Range • Streets of Laredo • The Yellow Rose of Texas • and more.
00699636 ....$19.99

Creedence Clearwater Revival
34 CCR classics: Bad Moon Rising • Born on the Bayou • Down on the Corner • Fortunate Son • Up Around the Bend • and more.
00701786 ....$16.99

Jim Croce
37 tunes: Bad, Bad Leroy Brown • I Got a Name • I'll Have to Say I Love You in a Song • Operator (That's Not the Way It Feels) • Photographs and Memories • Time in a Bottle • You Don't Mess Around with Jim • and many more.
00148087 ....$14.99

Crosby, Stills & Nash
37 hits: Chicago • Dark Star • Deja Vu • Marrakesh Express • Our House • Southern Cross • Suite: Judy Blue Eyes • Teach Your Children • and more.
00701609..............................$16.99

John Denver
50 favorites: Annie's Song • Leaving on a Jet Plane • Rocky Mountain High • Take Me Home, Country Roads • Thank God I'm a Country Boy • and more.
02501697 ....$17.99

Neil Diamond
50 songs: America • Cherry, Cherry • Cracklin' Rosie • Forever in Blue Jeans • I Am...I Said • Love on the Rocks • Song Sung Blue • Sweet Caroline • and dozens more!
00700606 ....$19.99

Disney
56 super Disney songs: Be Our Guest • Friend like Me • Hakuna Matata • It's a Small World • Under the Sea • A Whole New World • Zip-A-Dee-Doo-Dah • and more.
00701071 ....$17.99

The Doors
60 classics from the Doors: Break on Through to the Other Side • Hello, I Love You (Won't You Tell Me Your Name?) • Light My Fire • Love Her Madly • Riders on the Storm • Touch Me • and more.
00699888 ....$17.99

Eagles
40 familiar songs: Already Gone • Best of My Love • Desperado • Hotel California • Life in the Fast Lane • Peaceful Easy Feeling • Witchy Woman • more.
00122917 ....$16.99

Early Rock
80 classics: All I Have to Do Is Dream • Big Girls Don't Cry • Fever • Itsy Bitsy Teenie Weenie Yellow Polkadot Bikini • Let's Twist Again • Lollipop • and more.
00699916 ....$14.99

Folk Pop Rock
80 songs: American Pie • Dust in the Wind • Me and Bobby McGee • Somebody to Love • Time in a Bottle • and more.
00699651 ....$17.99

Folksongs
80 folk favorites: Aura Lee • Camptown Races • Danny Boy • Man of Constant Sorrow • Nobody Knows the Trouble I've Seen • and more.
00699541 ....$14.99

40 Easy Strumming Songs
Features 40 songs: Cat's in the Cradle • Daughter • Hey, Soul Sister • Homeward Bound • Take It Easy • Wild Horses • and more.
00115972 ....$16.99

Four Chord Songs
40 hit songs: Blowin' in the Wind • I Saw Her Standing There • Should I Stay or Should I Go • Stand by Me • Turn the Page • Wonderful Tonight • and more.
00701611 ....$14.99

Glee
50+ hits: Bad Romance • Beautiful • Dancing with Myself • Don't Stop Believin' • Imagine • Rehab • Teenage Dream • True Colors • and dozens more.
00702501 ....$14.99

Gospel Hymns
80 hymns: Amazing Grace • Give Me That Old Time Religion • I Love to Tell the Story • Shall We Gather at the River? • Wondrous Love • and more.
00700463 ....$14.99

Grand Ole Opry®
80 great songs: Abilene • Act Naturally • Country Boy • Crazy • Friends in Low Places • He Stopped Loving Her Today • Wings of a Dove • dozens more!
00699885 ....$16.95

Grateful Dead
30 favorites: Casey Jones • Friend of the Devil • High Time • Ramble on Rose • Ripple • Rosemary • Sugar Magnolia • Truckin' • Uncle John's Band • more.
00139461 ....$14.99

Green Day
34 faves: American Idiot • Basket Case • Boulevard of Broken Dreams • Good Riddance (Time of Your Life) • 21 Guns • Wake Me Up When September Ends • When I Come Around • and more.
00103074 ....$14.99

Irish Songs
45 Irish favorites: Danny Boy • Girl I Left Behind Me • Harrigan • I'll Tell Me Ma • The Irish Rover • My Wild Irish Rose • When Irish Eyes Are Smiling • and more!
00701044 ....$14.99

Michael Jackson
27 songs: Bad • Beat It • Billie Jean • Black or White (Rap Version) • Don't Stop 'Til You Get Enough • The Girl Is Mine • Man in the Mirror • Rock with You • Smooth Criminal • Thriller • more.
00137847 ....$14.99

Billy Joel
60 Billy Joel favorites: • It's Still Rock and Roll to Me • The Longest Time • Piano Man • She's Always a Woman • Uptown Girl • We Didn't Start the Fire • You May Be Right • and more.
00699632 ....$19.99

Elton John
60 songs: Bennie and the Jets • Candle in the Wind • Crocodile Rock • Goodbye Yellow Brick Road • Sad Songs Say So Much • Tiny Dancer • Your Song • more.
00699732 ....$15.99

Ray LaMontagne
20 songs: Empty • Gossip in the Grain • Hold You in My Arms • I Still Care for You • Jolene • Trouble • You Are the Best Thing • and more.
00130337..............................$12.99

Latin Songs
60 favorites: Bésame Mucho (Kiss Me Much) • The Girl from Ipanema (Garôta De Ipanema) • The Look of Love • So Nice (Summer Samba) • and more.
00700973 ....$14.99

Love Songs
65 romantic ditties: Baby, I'm-A Want You • Fields of Gold • Here, There and Everywhere • Let's Stay Together • Never My Love • The Way We Were • more!
00701043..............................$14.99

Bob Marley
36 songs: Buffalo Soldier • Get up Stand Up • I Shot the Sheriff • Is This Love • No Woman No Cry • One Love • Redemption Song • and more.
00701704..............................$17.99

Bruno Mars
15 hits: Count on Me • Grenade • If I Knew • Just the Way You Are • The Lazy Song • Locked Out of Heaven • Marry You • Treasure • When I Was Your Man • and more.
00125332 ....$12.99

Paul McCartney
60 from Sir Paul: Band on the Run • Jet • Let 'Em In • Maybe I'm Amazed • No More Lonely Nights • Say Say Say • Take It Away • With a Little Luck • and more!
00385035 ....$16.95

Steve Miller
33 hits: Dance Dance Dance • Jet Airliner • The Joker • Jungle Love • Rock'n Me • Serenade from the Stars • Swingtown • Take the Money and Run • and more.
00701146..............................$12.99

Modern Worship
80 modern worship favorites: All Because of Jesus • Amazed • Everlasting God • Happy Day • I Am Free • Jesus Messiah • and more.
00701801 ....$16.99

Motown
60 Motown masterpieces: ABC • Baby I Need Your Lovin' • I'll Be There • Stop! In the Name of Love • You Can't Hurry Love • and more.
00699734 ....$17.99

Willie Nelson
44 favorites: Always on My Mind • Beer for My Horses • Blue Skies • Georgia on My Mind • Help Me Make It Through the Night • On the Road Again • Whiskey River • and many more.
00148273 ....$17.99

Nirvana
40 songs: About a Girl • Come as You Are • Heart Shaped Box • The Man Who Sold the World • Smells like Teen Spirit • You Know You're Right • and more.
00699762 ....$16.99

Roy Orbison
38 songs: Blue Bayou • Oh, Pretty Woman • Only the Lonely (Know the Way I Feel) • Working for the Man • You Got It • and more.
00699752 ....$17.99

Peter, Paul & Mary
43 favorites: If I Had a Hammer (The Hammer Song) • Leaving on a Jet Plane • Puff the Magic Dragon • This Land Is Your Land • and more.
00103013..................................$19.99

Tom Petty
American Girl • Breakdown • Don't Do Me like That • Free Fallin' • Here Comes My Girl • Into the Great Wide Open • Mary Jane's Last Dance • Refugee • Runnin' Down a Dream • The Waiting • and more.
00699883 ....$15.99

Pink Floyd
30 songs: Another Brick in the Wall, Part 2 • Brain Damage • Breathe • Comfortably Numb • Hey You • Money • Mother • Run like Hell • Us and Them • Wish You Were Here • Young Lust • and many more.
00139116 ....$14.99

Pop/Rock
80 chart hits: Against All Odds • Come Sail Away • Every Breath You Take • Hurts So Good • Kokomo • More Than Words • Smooth • Summer of '69 • and more.
00699538 ....$16.99

Praise and Worship
80 favorites: Agnus Dei • He Is Exalted • I Could Sing of Your Love Forever • Lord, I Lift Your Name on High • More Precious Than Silver • Open the Eyes of My Heart • Shine, Jesus, Shine • and more.
00699634 ....$14.99

Elvis Presley
60 hits: All Shook Up • Blue Suede Shoes • Can't Help Falling in Love • Heartbreak Hotel • Hound Dog • Jailhouse Rock • Suspicious Minds • Viva Las Vegas • and more.
00699633 ....$17.99

Queen
40 hits: Bohemian Rhapsody • Crazy Little Thing Called Love • Fat Bottomed Girls • Killer Queen • Tie Your Mother Down • Under Pressure • You're My Best Friend • and more!
00702395 ....$14.99

Red Hot Chili Peppers
50 hits: Californication • Give It Away • Higher Ground • Love Rollercoaster • Scar Tissue • Suck My Kiss • Under the Bridge • and more.
00699710 ....$19.99

The Rolling Stones
35 hits: Angie • Beast of Burden • Fool to Cry • Happy • It's Only Rock 'N' Roll (But I Like It) • Miss You • Not Fade Away • Respectable • Rocks Off • Start Me Up • Time Is on My Side • Tumbling Dice • Waiting on a Friend • and more.
00137716 ....$17.99

Bob Seger
41 favorites: Against the Wind • Hollywood Nights • Katmandu • Like a Rock • Night Moves • Old Time Rock & Roll • You'll Accomp'ny Me • and more!
00701147..................................$12.99

Carly Simon
Nearly 40 classic hits, including: Anticipation • Haven't Got Time for the Pain • Jesse • Let the River Run • Nobody Does It Better • You're So Vain • and more.
00121011..................................$14.99

Sting
50 favorites from Sting and the Police: Don't Stand So Close to Me • Every Breath You Take • Fields of Gold • King of Pain • Message in a Bottle • Roxanne • and more.
00699921 ....$17.99

Taylor Swift
40 tunes: Back to December • Bad Blood • Blank Space • Fearless • Fifteen • I Knew You Were Trouble • Look What You Made Me Do • Love Story • Mean • Shake It Off • Speak Now • Wildest Dreams • and many more.
00263755..................................$16.99

Three Chord Acoustic Songs
30 acoustic songs: All Apologies • Blowin' in the Wind • Hold My Hand • Just the Way You Are • Ring of Fire • Shelter from the Storm • This Land Is Your Land • and more.
00123860 ....$14.99

Three Chord Songs
65 includes: All Right Now • La Bamba • Lay Down Sally • Mony, Mony • Rock Around the Clock • Rock This Town • Werewolves of London • You Are My Sunshine • and more.
00699720 ....$17.99

Two-Chord Songs
Nearly 60 songs: ABC • Brick House • Eleanor Rigby • Fever • Paperback Writer • Ramblin' Man Tulsa Time • When Love Comes to Town • and more.
00119236..................................$16.99

U2
40 U2 songs: Beautiful Day • Mysterious Ways • New Year's Day • One • Sunday Bloody Sunday • Walk On • Where the Streets Have No Name • With or Without You • and more.
00137744..................................$14.99

Hank Williams
68 classics: Cold, Cold Heart • Hey, Good Lookin' • Honky Tonk Blues • I'm a Long Gone Daddy • Jambalaya (On the Bayou) • Your Cheatin' Heart • and more.
00700607 ....$16.99

Stevie Wonder
40 of Stevie's best: For Once in My Life • Higher Ground • Isn't She Lovely • My Cherie Amour • Sir Duke • Superstition • Uptight (Everything's Alright) • Yester-Me, Yester-You, Yesterday • and more!
00120862 ....$14.99

HAL•LEONARD®

Prices, contents and availability subject to change without notice.

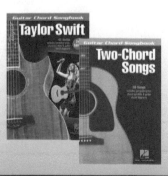

Complete contents listings available online at www.halleonard.com

1120; 6/9; 121